The Path of the
DreamHealer

Also by Adam

DreamHealer: A True Story of Miracle Healings

DreamHealer 2: A Guide to Healing and Self-Empowerment

The Path of the
DreamHealer

*My Journey
Through the
Miraculous
World of
Energy
Healing*

ADAM

DUTTON

DUTTON
Published by Penguin Group
Penguin Group (USA) Inc., 375 Hudson Street, New York, New York 10014, U.S.A.
Penguin Group (Canada), 90 Eglinton Avenue East, Suite 700, Toronto, Ontario M4P 2Y3,
Canada (a division of Pearson Penguin Canada Inc.)
Penguin Books Ltd., 80 Strand, London WC2R 0RL, England
Penguin Ireland, 25 St. Stephen's Green, Dublin 2, Ireland (a division of Penguin Books Ltd.)
Penguin Group (Australia), 250 Camberwell Road, Camberwell, Victoria 3124, Australia
(a division of Pearson Australia Group Pty. Ltd.)
Penguin Books India Pvt. Ltd., 11 Community Centre, Panchsheel Park,
New Delhi – 110 017, India
Penguin Books (NZ), cnr Airborne and Rosedale Roads, Albany, Auckland 1310,
New Zealand (a division of Pearson New Zealand Ltd.)
Penguin Books (South Africa) (Pty.) Ltd., 24 Sturdee Avenue, Rosebank,
Johannesburg 2196, South Africa

Penguin Books Ltd., Registered Offices: 80 Strand, London WC2R 0RL, England

First published in March 2006 by Viking Canada

Published by Dutton, a member of Penguin Group (USA) Inc.

First U.S. printing, July 2006
1 3 5 7 9 10 8 6 4 2

Copyright © 2006 by DreamHealer Inc.

All rights reserved

REGISTERED TRADEMARK-MARCA—REGISTRADA

LIBRARY OF CONGRESS CATALOGING-IN-PUBLICATION DATA
has been applied for.

ISBN 0-525-94948-8

Printed in the United States of America
Set in Minion

While the author has made every effort to provide accurate telephone numbers and Internet addresses at the time of publication, neither the publisher nor the author assumes any responsibility for errors, or for changes that occur after publication. Further, the publisher does not have any control over and does not assume any responsibility for the author or third-party Web sites or their content.

In memory of my cat Gizmo,
my good friend

Contents

Contents

The
Path
of
the
DreamHealer

From Outer Space to Inner Space

I have been given the gift of being an energy healer in this life-time. I have been drawn to healing people and to helping them achieve self-empowerment. My goal is to teach others how to use their innate energy resources and intentions to heal themselves and others. This has been the focus of my practice, my work-shops and my two previous books. This book continues to focus on healing. It is about our beginnings and our characteristics and abilities as energy beings.

Concepts such as the Big Bang, biophotons, consciousness and reincarnation are all related to our health and healing. Although these concepts and others are explained in scientific terms in this book, it is not intended as a science textbook. Rather, *The Path of the DreamHealer* is a compilation of the information I have received and learned through intuition— part of my gift is being able to intuitively receive huge amounts of information that is normally acquired through years of study and research. Many people refer to this process of "downloading" information intuitively as channeling. I in turn have acted as a conduit in that these concepts have been channeled through me to you. All of the information I receive intuitively is in the form of complex scientific images, but here I have simplified the science to make it as accessible to readers as possible.

While it is not necessary to understand the details of quantum physics in order to practice self-healing, it is useful to have a general understanding of where energy comes from and how it works. I provide a general overview of this in Part 1, "How It All Began," which includes the story of my journey to affirm a vision I had. It is one of my most powerful examples of my unusual experiences and the one underlying the "downloading" of the information which is the basis of this book. So just how is the origin of our universe related to health and healing? As I discuss in Chapter 2, everything in the universe is energy, whether in the form of a wave or a particle. Moreover, everything in the universe originated from a common energy source. According to the Big Bang theory, the dominant scientific theory about the origin of the universe, the universe was created some-time between ten billion and fifteen billion years ago when a cosmic explosion hurled matter in all directions. Because of this, we are all energetically connected as one. We all have access to all of the knowledge in the universe; that knowledge is in the form of energy. This means we can access the information needed for healing. We do this through our intuition and intentions. The "library" of this universal knowledge is commonly referred to as "the field." In Chapter 3, I discuss the access that each of us has to this field, while the meditation exercises and self-healing visualizations you'll find in Part 3 of this book will help you tap into this universal field of information.

⌒

My gift was revealed to me in a variety of ways as I was growing up. As far back as I can remember I saw auras, the subtle light surrounding all living things. As I didn't know differently, I thought this was normal. It wasn't until my early teenage years that I realized this is an unusual ability. Furthermore, telekinetic events occurred around me that could not easily be dismissed as typical. When objects I reached for shot off away from me and my pencil flew out of my hand and hit the blackboard at school, I became very curious. (And it was nearly impossible to convince my teacher that I wasn't throwing things.)

Then one day, my mom was in excruciating pain from trigeminal neuralgia, an affliction caused by her multiple sclerosis. I told her to close her eyes and I placed my hand on her head. I wasn't thinking about anything in particular; I just didn't want my mom to be in pain anymore. I saw a throbbing bright green blob in her head. I grabbed it and pulled it out into me. "That was a horrible pain that you had," I said aloud. My mom was immediately pain-free, but I had taken on her stabbing headache. That was the last trigeminal neuralgia pain she ever had. By morning I felt fine, but my parents were very concerned.

What had happened? Was my health now at risk? I too was baffled. Fortunately, through practice and some guidance, I soon learned how to influence another person's health without taking on his or her symptoms.

This started my most interesting journey on the path of healing. I didn't know how healing worked, but I knew there was much more to our universe than we can perceive with our five physical senses. Then I heard that *Apollo 14* astronaut Edgar Mitchell was coming to town to speak at a meeting of the Institute of Noetic Sciences (IONS), of which he is the founder. On Dr. Mitchell's return journey to earth, he became aware of a deep sense of universal connectedness. Having had this transformational experience in space, he decided to devote his life to finding scientific explanations for unusual or little understood phenomena. At the time, I was aware that I could see health information about a person and that I could influence it, but I had no scientific terms for or understanding of what I was accessing. From attending the IONS meeting and afterward speaking to Dr. Mitchell, I learned that the information I was seeing was described scientifically as the hologram of the person's energy field. Furthermore, some quantum physicists were describing what they perceived to be a holographic universe, in which every part of the universe, including each of us, contains all of the information of the universe. This concept resonated with how I experience my healing work. My meeting with Dr. Mitchell was no coincidence, and he has been my science mentor ever since.

Shortly after, I started writing *DreamHealer*, which describes an experiential view of distant healing. Although the academic theory of quantum physics is discussed (in simple terms), the focus of the book is on self-discovery, and an understanding of our own awareness as we seek to achieve a higher level of consciousness.

Following the publication of *DreamHealer*, I became aware that readers want more information on how they can positively impact their own health. So I wrote *DreamHealer 2: A Guide to Healing and Self-Empowerment*, providing details on visualizations and other tools that will help readers practice self-healing. My step-by-step instructions show how to activate the immune system and return the body, mind and spirit to its natural balance and state of well-being.

When I look at someone, I see the person's body enveloped in energy of flowing colors. This is the outer reflection of the energetic system, or aura, which surrounds all living things. While playing basketball one day, I observed that intention affects a person's aura: When another player thought about passing the ball, this intention registered as a small spike on his aura in the direction he wanted to pass it. This allowed me to better anticipate my opponent's play and intercept the ball. This is when I fully realized the power of intention.

Some healing arts focus on the aura. In healthy areas of the body, the aura moves and swirls in a pattern and appears organized and in harmony: There is a flow. In an afflicted area, this flow is broken. Healers use their hands and minds to smooth and repair the energy blockages negatively affecting the body. I can get a great deal of information from the aura because it is evident from them where blockages of energy in the body are: These stagnant areas pinpoint the locations of existing or developing problems. But my vision goes much deeper than the aura. I have the ability to see energy fields at many different frequencies, which enables me to do a type of body scan on a person.

As I learned at the IONS meeting, a scientific concept that relates directly to how I practice healing is the hologram—a three-dimensional projection containing all of the information (past, present and future) of a person, place or thing, including, with people, their optimal state of health. This projection appears before me in the form of an image. Some scientists speculate that because the universe is holographic—meaning the universe is just information—our brains also operate and interact with the universal energy field holographically. Given our interconnectedness, we are all connected to this oneness of information.

You may be a little bit familiar with holograms if you have ever worn the three-dimensional glasses in a theater that project what looks like a holographic image of what is on the movie screen. You can see that images look like they are hanging in space. With holograms, every piece of that image contains all of the information of the whole image. This is typical of laser-created holograms, where each part of the holographic material contains the entire image, even if it is shattered into many pieces. So too in a holographic universe: Every particle of the universe, every cell of our bodies, every neuron in our brains contains all of the information in the universe. It's astonishing to imagine the resources we have at our disposal. It makes sense, then, when neuroscientists tell us that we use only a fraction of our brain power.

Each of us emits a hologram containing all information about us. Everyone is connected to the field of information by their unique body frequency—the frequency or resonance of the energy or light of their body. Like tuning a radio station to a particular frequency, I am able to tune in to a person's frequency within the field of information. At first, everything around me goes dark, then I "see" a holographic image of the person's body. I call this process "going in," as I can "see" an X-ray–type view in great detail. On this image, I can see areas of injuries or illness. When I am connected to the person, I also pick up a lot of intuitive information about the person, for example, what his or her attitudes and beliefs are. This helps me to see the energy blockages and, through my intention—that is, my intention to heal—manipulate energy to clear these blockages, permitting energy to flow harmoniously and, thus, allow the body to change. It is important to remember that we are all connected because we are all energy. If you view matter in its smallest manifestation, you would not find solid matter. Our interconnection to one another can be thought of as an ocean of energy. Like every atom in an ocean of water, every bit of energy is connected. If you throw a rock into an ocean, that rock and its impact will affect every atom in that ocean, as one molecule is connected to and influencing all others.

I also have the ability to zoom in to the hologram or access different layers to work on. For instance, if I want to look at the pancreas, I can go straight to the level where I can see all the fluids flowing within that gland. With my healing intention, I can tune in to and "see" any number of subsets of information contained within the hologram. Through my intentions to influence, I can control what information I receive about a particular health concern. This is similar to operating a remote control to access different television stations. My mind acts as a remote control that can adjust to different sets of frequencies, giving me different holographic views.

I can zero in on electrical impulses between neurons in the brain, or see specific systems of the body, such as neurological and skeletal, as well as that of the organs. The various holographic views of the body are like the various blueprints used in the construction of a building. There is a floor plan, electrical drawings and plumbing schematics of the same structure. Which view of the body is most useful simply depends on what part of the body or ailment I intend to focus on.

Through intention, I am able to create a resonance, or common energy frequency, between healing information I am projecting to interact with that person's hologram and me. Because our bodies are constantly interacting with their environments through the exchange of information, the person with whom I am interacting progressively reflects these healing changes.

An important concept that relates to my distant healing abilities is nonlocality, commonly referred to as quantum action-at-a-distance. A quantum object simultaneously influences its correlated twin object, no matter how far apart they are. This explains how energy can influence other energy elsewhere, and therefore why geographical distance or proximity is not a factor.

Photons, the smallest physical units of light, are capable of transferring information universally. Biophotons are the photons that are emitted from every living cell or organism. These electromagnetic frequencies (discussed in more detail in Part 1) are all energy or ways of describing energy.

In the quantum world, which is the world defined in terms of the smallest realizable units, the act of simply observing or interacting with a quantum object changes its behavior. Physicists readily acknowledge that they do not understand many of these aspects of the quantum world, but their mathematical formulas verify quantum theory. But what still perplexes physicists is why that quantum object's quantum twin simultaneously changes, no matter how far apart the quantum object and its twin are. Some refer to this connection as "entanglement."

Because of the connection of everything to everything else, our thoughts and intentions can influence events nonlocally. This quantum attribute of nonlocality helps me understand how I can facilitate a person's healing from a distance: I am able to connect to a person's frequency and see his or her hologram simply by looking at a photograph of that person's face.

When I do my distant healing, the transfer of information in the field is not affected by time and space. I know this because the clarity of information I receive from someone 5000 miles away is the same as if the person were in the next room. For example, I have connected to someone in China for a treatment and the distance made no difference to the treatment's effectiveness. In another case, my uncle showed me a photograph of a man and asked me what I saw. I had never seen anything like it. His skeletal holographic image was stretched and elongated. I told my uncle what I saw and asked what ailment the man had. My uncle replied that the photo was of a cosmonaut aboard the International Space Station as it orbited a hundred miles above the earth. No wonder that his hologram, when he was in reduced gravity, appeared a little peculiar to me.

⌒⌐

How do we relate all of the information in the field to our present reality? I address this question in Part 2 by discussing the more personal and metaphysical aspects of this oneness and interconnectedness as it relates to our health. What role do our beliefs and emotions play? How does universal energy manifest itself in consciousness, reincarnation, karma and past lives? These metaphysical concepts help us understand more clearly our self-healing abilities. Chapter 6 includes exercises to help you access more effectively these innate healing skills that we all possess.

As an energy healer, I work with the properties of energy. You, as your own self-healer, can also learn to work with these properties. In addition to science mentors, I have had the pleasure of working with people from alternative healing disciplines, including qigong masters, Reiki masters and shamans from many indigenous cultures. I've also worked with people who have discovered their healing abilities on their own. Every healer within each discipline has learned different ways to access a similar ability. What I have learned is that each and every one of us naturally possesses this healing capacity. Most of us just need some simple directions as to how to maximize our awareness of it and focus our intentions to guide it.

Throughout the book, I emphasize the powerful effect our beliefs and expectations have on our health. I have seen many people with varying beliefs as I go about my work. I feel that everyone is entitled to his or her beliefs, and my purpose is simply to respond to needs as I am able. However, in my experience, it makes a huge difference if the recipient of energy treatments understands what is happening and participates in his or her own healing. My objective in healing is to teach people how to effectively improve their own health through their own intervention.

Most people with paranormal abilities would love to find some scientific means of proving what they are experiencing. My parents were no different. They were eager to consult with experts who could answer some of their questions. They thought that contacting research experts at a reputable university would be a good place to start. This was the beginning of our experience as a family understanding the resistance that is found in the academic world. The professors we talked to were skeptics. We had hoped to find someone with an open mind who was willing to consider our questions about the paranormal with the intent of understanding rather than disproving these phenomena.

It is healthy to be an open-minded skeptic. However, those who proudly label themselves skeptics may be creating and reinforcing paradigms that prevent them from being open to understanding events beyond that of our five senses.

Since discovering my ability to influence health, I have been overwhelmed with requests for help. As I contemplated how to respond to such a great need, I realized that it is possible to join auras in a group of similarly intentioned people and affect change. From observing how intention affects auras, the idea came to me to do group energy treatments so that more people could benefit. This presented me with wonderful possibilities. I began leading workshops to teach people how to influence their health through intention.

Everything is connected at its most basic form of energy. We are all truly one. In group treatments, I act as the conductor in the symphony of merging frequencies. Participants have the opportunity to experience what an energy treatment feels like and can learn how to do energy treatments for themselves. Given some simple tools, all group participants can learn to feel, and even see, subtle energy movement within and around the body and become comfortable taking this knowledge with them to continue their own self-healing.

I also realized that when people participate in their own healing, a lasting change occurs. People feel incredible strength when they are empowered to do their own healing, when they realize that they have the tools to positively influence their own health physically, emotionally and spiritually.

When facilitating a group treatment, I am in a trancelike state of consciousness in which I am not fully aware of my physical surroundings. When returning to ordinary consciousness, my experience is similar to emerging out of a cave into brilliant sunshine. My pupils are fully dilated so my eyes take time to adjust to the light, even in a darkened room. Directing energy is energy consuming. After a group treatment, I find that my mind muscle has been thoroughly exercised. I rebalance myself by exercising my physical body.

Many people who have connected to me through the reading of my books or attending one of my workshops have written to me that they have visualized me when they are in a dream state. Upon meeting someone face-to-face, or even connecting at a distance, a bond is formed. We forge an even stronger bond if our thoughts and intentions are aligned. We feel this connection in a group treatment through our mutual experience and what we share. The barriers of individualism we have erected are nothing more than facades. A global shift in consciousness will erode these barriers as our evolution continues.

Many aspects of energy healing and other alternative disciplines have been seen as mysterious, shrouded in secrecy and ritual. My hope is that the discussion in this book of the energy concepts will help demystify the healing process. The self-healing strategies, in the form of visualization exercises, will help you learn how to heal yourself. The visualizations can be customized to meet your particular health challenge. Every one of us has different strengths and sensitivities. Our five senses vary in dominance. Some people are very visual, others are auditory and some feel everything intensely. We need to be aware of our individual strengths and use them to our advantage. You can tailor visualizations to your particular strengths and preferences, such as using primarily visual or primarily auditory input.

Just know that you have self-healing ability. The source of energy used in an energy treatment is the limitless energy of the universe. It is attracted by our boundless imagination and guided by positive healing intentions. Our thoughts and intentions, which are energetic phenomena, are unlimited. When you have a grasp of what science is suggesting about the origin of the universe and you understand your experiences as both a material (solidified energy) and nonmaterial (wavelike energy) being, you may be willing to open your mind to the power of energy and intention. I urge you to explore the ability that all of us have to influence our own health.

PART I

How It All Began

Chapter I
The Vision

The only limits that you have are the limits which you have set for yourself in your own mind.

—ADAM

Several years ago I had my first vision. It was an incredibly vivid dream where I was soaring above the ocean like an eagle. Then I found myself running very quickly through a forest. Suddenly, all motion came to a halt. Then I saw a big black bird sitting atop a mound of earth. I then got a strong feeling that I had to go to Nootka. I had never heard of Nootka and so had no idea where it was.

I told my parents about this vision and that I had a strong feeling that we had to go to Nootka. We went to the library to do some research. We discovered that Nootka Sound, also called Friendly Cove, is a remote area on the west side of Vancouver Island, in British Columbia, and is where Captain Cook first set anchor on his second expedition of the Northwest Coast. I found this particularly interesting, since I am related to Captain Cook on my mom's side. Through my dad, I am part Penobscot, a Native American band based on the east coast of the United States. Nootka Sound is a historical meeting place of both sides of my family roots: European and Native American. The pictures of the Nootka region in the library books looked familiar to me. I recognized the landscape and, pointing to one particular picture, exclaimed, "That's where we have to go." My dad asked, "What will we be looking for when we arrive?" I replied that I had to find the big black bird which I had seen in my vision. Since summer was approaching, we decided to make a family vacation of this trip. We learned that Nootka Sound is accessible only by seaplane or boat. Then we learned that a converted minesweeper delivers supplies to the island lighthouse twice a week and also carries travelers back and forth for a day trip.

My grandparents and uncle heard about our trip plans and decided to join us. Although everyone except my younger sister knew of the many unusual events such as pencils flying that had occurred around me, I had told only my mom and dad about the details of the vision. But my grandparents and uncle knew I had had a vision of some sort and they understood that Nootka Sound was a place I needed to go in order to follow my vision. So we all got together with our calendars to set the travel date. The first date that suited all of us happened to be my sixteenth birthday. Without thinking, I said to my mom, "That's good because although it is going to be really cloudy in the morning, it will be sunny when we arrive." My mom did not say anything about my weather prediction but remembered it because, considering how variable West Coast weather is, it is hard enough to make an accurate weather prediction for the next day, let alone six weeks in advance.

During our planning for the trip, I noticed that two crows seemed to be always following me. They woke me up every morning and were more or less permanent fixtures in our yard. They followed me to the tennis courts and sat atop the fence. But I didn't spend any time trying to understand their presence. Then, several days before our trip, they were nowhere to be seen.

Our journey began with a two-hour ferry ride to Vancouver Island and then a four-hour drive inland to the town of Gold River. When we arrived at our motel, two crows sitting on the telephone wire at its entrance cawed in greeting.

We didn't need to board the minesweeper that would take us to Nootka Sound until the next morning, so we decided to visit some nearby caves that had been known to the Native people of the area for centuries. As we drove down the long, winding dirt road back toward the town, after having explored the caves, one of the two crows guided us along. It flew only a few feet in front of our windshield most of the way back, leading us through every twist and turn of the road. We were all amazed.

In the late afternoon, we stopped at a sandy spot on the river bank to have a swim, since it was a hot, cloudless day. My mom reminded me of the weather prediction I had made weeks ago for the next day. It seemed unlikely to her that it would be cloudy for our journey, as I had seen in my vision.

The next morning we woke up early. Overhead, there was a solid blanket of clouds and it felt like a November day, even though it was July. We all bundled up in layers of clothing and headed out to the old minesweeper.

We boarded along with about fifty other campers, tourists and adventurers. The galley did a booming business serving steaming hot chocolate and chili to all of the shivering travelers on deck. I told my mom not to be concerned about the weather. As in my vision, it would be hot and sunny when we arrived. She looked up at the massive, dark clouds and said, "Whatever. As long as it doesn't rain, we'll be all right."

The scenery was spectacular as we headed through the ocean waters toward Nootka Sound. Halfway to our destination, a single orca approached the boat. The whale followed alongside the boat for a long time, breaching and tail slapping. We learned that this male orca, which had become separated from its pod the year before, had been named Luna by some of the locals. The local Native Americans called him Tsuux-iit. Most passengers busied themselves taking photographs of the orca. I hoped that he would some day be reunited with his pod.

To the west, we saw a patch of clear blue sky. The clouds looked like a blanket being peeled back. A moment later we could see the lighthouse near the dock. Just then, brilliant summer sun emerged. We quickly stuffed our jackets and sweaters into our backpacks and prepared to disembark. I could see what appeared to me as a searchlight beam shining in the woods beyond the dock, and I was eager to begin on the adventure that was about to unfold. The captain announced that the boat would be leaving and returning to the mainland in three hours with or without us.

Even before the boat was secured to the dock, I leapt off and began running toward the light beam. My dad hurried after me. A path parallel to the water led us through an ancient Native burial ground. I was awestruck to think of the meeting of two such different cultures hundreds of years ago at this very site where Captain Cook first landed, but for now I needed to focus on my vision. Part way along the path I told my dad that we had to veer off the trail. This meant making our way through ferns and several feet of undergrowth in the dense West Coast forest.

After we ventured about a hundred yards into the forest, we stopped and scanned the area. My dad said, "There isn't anything here." I replied, "I know that it's here because I can feel it."

Then we saw the bird about fifty feet in front of us (see Illustration 1). It was four feet tall, black, with piercing black eyes, just like in my vision. We walked toward it until we were within twenty feet of it. As I locked eyes with it, it telepathically delivered complex scientific information to me in the form of images. The amount of information and the delivery speed were analogous to watching many hours of a video recording in just seconds. I told my dad that the human brain wasn't meant to take in so much information. Then the bird reverted from being the messenger to being just a bird again. This was obvious to me, as I began to telepathically receive "A day in the life of a bird" images, such as what it ate for breakfast.

Once my dad decided that I was okay while experiencing such an awesome event, he went looking for my mom, who was nearby, walking along the shoreline. Dad led her to where I was and pointed to the bird without saying anything. My mom remarked at what an odd location it was for a totem pole.

As my mom got closer to the bird, she saw its eyes blink and she came to a halt. She shivered and all the hairs on the back of her neck stood up at the realization that the bird was alive. I knew that the bird did not intend to hurt us or it would have attacked already. It was clear to me that it was there for some other reason.

After a few minutes, my mom left and shortly afterward returned with my grandparents and uncle. All were rendered speechless by what they saw. We took some photographs. The bird remained in the same spot the entire time, only ruffling its feathers when someone got too close for its comfort. It was such a beautiful sight that we all were in awe. Then we had to return to the boat, as three hours were nearly up.

On the voyage back to Gold River, we found it difficult to even talk about what we had seen, as it seemed so incredible and beyond words. We were all stunned by the experience. What a sixteenth birthday it had been for me.

The next morning, my dad was chatting with the local Native chief and he asked him about the bird we had seen. The chief said he didn't know of any large black birds in the area. He had seen some large ravens, but not as big as the one we described.

On the drive from Gold River to the ferry back home, we stopped in at a Native souvenir shop. Near its entrance stood one fairly large totem pole. A figure of a large black bird was carved at the top. I asked the shop's clerk about the bird and its habitat. She told me that it was the mythical thunderbird.

The presence of this large black bird in the exact location that I had seen in my vision had huge significance for me. It confirmed that the extraordinary events I had been experiencing for several years were real; I myself was unsure of my experiences, but when my vision manifested physically, all my doubts were eliminated. I could trust myself on my way forward, and my family was able to justify their support of me. After the vision, I no longer had any doubts within me; this greatly amplified my healing abilities and made me open to receiving through intuition much more information from the field. It gave me the confidence I needed at that time.

I downloaded so much complex information from the bird into my consciousness that, several years later, there is still much that I have not been able to decipher. And it wasn't a finite amount of information that I received. Rather, the encounter with the bird opened a gateway in me that allows a more efficient connection to knowledge from the field of information. From that point onward, I have been constantly bombarded with vast amounts of information. This information comes to me in various forms. Sometimes it's words, sometimes images, sometimes thoughts, sometimes I hear a voice. It varies depending on the type of information.

Whether what I saw in the forest that day was a raven, an eagle or a mythical thunderbird is not the point. What is important is that the bird was there in all its magnificence, just as I had foreseen. I started believing in myself. This was the beginning of my journey, a journey that has taken me to write this book.

Did the bird make any sounds?

It made a clicking sound, something like the velociraptor in the movie *Jurassic Park*.

How far away were you from the bird?

We got as close as twenty feet to it. At this point, the bird showed signs of agitation: It made clicking noises and spread its wings slightly. We then backed away, as we didn't want to irritate it.

Did the bird move?

The bird stayed in the same location the entire time that we were there. It was there for at least an hour but eventually we had to leave because the boat was leaving.

Chapter 2
The Origin of the Universe

We all originate from a common energy,
which explains our interconnectedness.

—ADAM

After my vision I had the confidence to trust the information that I intuitively received. A lot of information that I was receiving was related to the science behind my unusual experiences. One day I felt compelled to write down some of this information that was pouring into my mind and distracting me from everything else. I went into my bedroom and within an hour had written down fifteen pages of scientific information which seemed to just flow out from me. That information now forms the basis of this chapter.

Humans have long sought to understand the origin of the universe and the origin and nature of consciousness. How did the universe originate? Has consciousness existed from the beginning, or has it evolved from something else? At first glance, a discussion about the origin of the universe may seem remote from healing, but in fact the two topics are strongly linked.

Imagine a time before the Big Bang, the cosmic explosion that occurred sometime between ten billion and fifteen billion years ago, hurling matter in all directions and thus creating the universe. All that existed prior to this event was energy constantly flowing in a seemingly random fashion, yet synchronized at some level. This simple state of energy had been flowing for an infinite length of time. With no physical matter in existence, there was an unlimited amount of empty space.

However, empty space is not really empty at all. Rather, it is a vacuum devoid of all physical matter but full of quantum energy fluctuations, that is, spontaneous movements of energy. Scientists have theorized that there is enough energy in one cup of empty space to boil all the oceans on earth. Energy is present in the form of waves, meaning it ripples outward like ripples in a pond, radiating in all directions.

Ripples or quantum fluctuations of energy have an effect on each other. Random pulses of energy interact as they bounce off or intersect with each other. Imagine watching ripples in the pond during a rainstorm. Sometimes the ripples converge and form a larger ripple. When ripples converge, the waves can amplify each other. Similarly, energy fluctuations accumulate at intersections, thereby increasing the concentration of energy in a specific area.

When there is a higher concentration of energy in a particular region of space, the probability of a quantum particle being manifested from energy fluctuations is increased (see Illustration 2). The probability of quantum fluctuations intersecting in the specific way necessary to produce matter is infinitesimally small, but there was an infinite amount of time before the Big Bang.

When the fluctuations did intersect in a specific way, the first quantum particle was created, and the Big Bang occurred. Since the Big Bang occurred instantly, rather than being a long process, it is more accurate to say that we all originate from a common energy event rather than from a particle.

I have often heard people ask, how can something come from nothing? But this question implies that matter is something and energy is nothing. This could not be further from the truth. When matter is broken down, it is simply energy. Scientists have mathematically proven that a particle can be manifested from the energy fluctuations in so-called empty space. Recently, physicists have demonstrated this theory by generating a particle solely out of such energy: They have shown it is possible to generate "something" from "nothing."

The mechanism that initiated and drove the Big Bang and that continues to drive the evolution of the universe is actually quite simple. The catalyst was gravity, which is the physical force that attracts particles to each other. With the manifestation of the first particle came the phenomenon of gravitational force (see Illustration 3). Although the first matter may have been only a tiny subatomic particle, its small gravitational field was enough to instantly initiate the Big Bang. Before this point, there was no gravitational field because there was no matter, and gravity doesn't exist without matter. As gravity attracted more energy, more particles manifested. As the number of particles increased, so did the gravitational pull, attracting even more energy.

All matter is simply energy oriented in such a way that it forms a bend in the space-time continuum. Bends in space-time cause the attraction of particles and a distortion in time. Time passes more slowly around a strong gravitational field than a weak one. If it were possible for someone to go very close to a black hole, time would pass slower for that person than someone who was farther away from it. A black hole is such a concentrated mass that gravity prevents anything from escaping from it. Extreme gravitational forces distort time very noticeably. Even small subatomic particles distort time and affect gravity in a similar way, although much more subtly than a black hole.

Albert Einstein described gravity by using the analogy of depressions in a mattress. After the creation of the first quantum particle, the previously level space-time continuum had a slight depression, making it no longer perfectly level. The mattress analogy is very useful for understanding how gravity works. An object in space, such as a meteor, has a tendency to fall back to earth, just as an object on the end of a mattress has a tendency to roll toward the depression.

Energy has the tendency to collect in this depression in space. The energy collected there tends to take on similar properties to that of the original space-time bending energy when it comes in close proximity to it. This will in turn cause the small space-time bend to increase. The more the bend increases, the faster it collects more energy. As more energy collects around this particle, more particles are created, in a dominolike effect. As more particles are created, the bend or depression becomes deeper, attracting more energy.

This process happens at a phenomenal rate. When the particles are initially manifested, they are at a very high temperature. Because of this, they have a very high velocity, and so rapidly burst out from their point of origin. These escaping particles then initiate the same process over again. It is quite easy to see how this could accelerate exponentially. Newly formed particles start shooting out particles. When a particle gets forced out, it creates its own depression, thus repeating the process.

What ended the process the Big Bang initiated? As more particles are manifested, the empty space surrounding these particles slowly becomes depleted of its energy. This energy did not disappear; however, it was simply transformed into matter. Of course, empty space never becomes completely exhausted of its energy, but it becomes depleted to the point where it can no longer spontaneously manifest particles. This is why if I place an object in a vacuum, I am not going to initiate another Big Bang.

This raises an interesting point. The "empty space" within the known universe must be different from the "empty space" outside our universe. Logically, the empty space within the universe contains less energy because some of the energy has been converted to matter. The empty space outside the universe contains more energy, as it has not converted any energy into matter. I refer to this space beyond our known universe as virgin space. The border between these two types of space is very gradual, likely billions of light years. Of course, there is no known way to confirm that there is a difference in the two types of space until we find a way to travel to the edge of the universe.

While there is still much we don't know about our universe, the most important concept to understand about the origin of the universe is that everything is interconnected. If you were able to freeze time just prior to the Big Bang, you would see that for an instant only one common energy—one singularity—existed. Everything in the universe originated from this singularity, and therefore everything in the universe shares a connection to everything else. The result is our web of interconnectedness. The term for this web of interconnected frequencies connecting all of the information in the universe is "the field of information." Any change in one event in this web affects the whole web or universe; everyone and everything is linked. You are one with the universe.

This interconnectedness explains your fundamental ability to influence your life and consequently your health. Think of this interconnecting web of energy and information in a comforting way. Imagine the threads of interconnectivity forming a hammock in which you can relax. The webbing holds you and enfolds you easily and comfortably.

Why did nature produce a Big Bang in the first place?
One of the basic laws of the universe is that everything always seeks the state of minimal energy. The Big Bang occurred in an

effort to reach minimal energy. It was energetically favorable for the Big Bang to occur as a result of a rare complex interaction from the energy in empty space before the Big Bang.

Can energy exist without matter?

Energy can exist without matter, as it did before the Big Bang. Matter is simply a form of energy. The quantum model of the atom shows that there is nothing tangible in matter: Matter does not exist but is simply energy vibrations. Energy did not magically appear at some point in time: It always was and always will be present in empty space. This energy keeps space stable.

Did time exist before the Big Bang?

Yes, time existed prior to the Big Bang; however, there was no matter in existence to reference time. All that existed was the energy fluctuations of empty space. Energy, of course, does not necessarily move in any predictable manner with regard to time. That is why it is difficult to reference time before the Big Bang.

Chapter 3
The Field of Information

*The field is a vast sea of information
without boundaries or separations.*

—ADAM

*O*ften I spontaneously pick up information from the field. When I go into a person's holographic information in order to heal, along with seeing the health concern, I also intuitively pick up related data. For instance, I examined a man with severe back pain. He had been to see the orthopedic surgeon several days before and was considering surgery to fuse his spine. I told him that the problem was lateral instability and drew a diagram of the problem to illustrate it. He was flabbergasted. Not only was the illustration exactly the same as the one the doctor had sketched for him just days before, but "lateral instability" were the exact words the doctor had used to describe his back problem. This information was data I had intuitively picked up. The man decided not to have the surgery, and I continued with my energy treatment on him. Now, years later, this man's back has not bothered him since.

The field where I accessed this information is the cumulative collection of all information about everything in the universe and its connection to everything else. The field includes all places and all times simultaneously: It includes links to past, present and all possible future events; it therefore contains all possible outcomes. The field provides a template for this information exchange. Think of it as an infinite sea that transcends all space between matter, energy and time.

The field existed before the Big Bang, when only quantum fluctuations and no matter existed, but in a very simple form. With the occurrence of the Big Bang, this field of information became increasingly dynamic and complex as matter created more matter.

To again use the analogy of a radio, imagine your mind as a radio receiver that is tuning in to various frequencies. You are able to select from many stations, and which one you choose depends on your desire—news, weather, sports or music. You adjust the dial until the reception is as clear as possible. Once you have tuned in to a particular station, you aren't able to hear the other stations, yet you know they exist. The field is similar in that all of the information you need is available to you; the information you access depends on your particular need. The visualizations I suggest in Part 3 are one way to access and use information from the field.

Usually, I access health information by using a face photograph of a person, connecting through the eyes. This is the most effective access point for me. However, information is everywhere. Some people make a connection through voice, such as a phone call. Sometimes I do too, although this is not a connection I can depend on.

My mom received a phone call from a man interested in my healing techniques. While she was on the phone with him, I walked in from another room. She asked me if I would do a treatment on the man. I asked for his name and when I got the reply, I blurted out, "The sciatic nerve is involved and that is why his leg is so painful. I don't see any more cancer though."

My mom didn't know at that point what the man's health challenge was, and she repeated to him exactly what I had said. For several moments he was speechless. Then he confirmed that he had just had a cancerous growth removed from his leg and it had been wrapped around his sciatic nerve.

We all have access to the same information. An infinite amount of information is passing through you at any given time. Your brain acts as the filtering mechanism by constantly selecting the information that it determines relevant. This is how we instantaneously decipher and analyze the incoming signals to obtain information that is useful to us. It must be decoded to be meaningful.

We all are equally connected to the field. This makes us truly one within this dynamic web of connectivity. A self separate from everyone else is an illusionary concept, created merely for our own purposes of human definition or for convenience. We must realize that we are all energy from the same source and that our individual realities are subjective. You can influence how you perceive your reality in any way you wish.

The field is the archive of universal information on both microscopic and macroscopic levels. It assists in the coordination of every cell within our bodies in order for the cells to exchange intelligent data. Even our growth and thought patterns are part of this communication, as well as memory, emotions and health issues. The field also contains all data about the planets and all celestial bodies in our universe, including the first quantum fluctuation. From the smallest subatomic particle to the immense, the field connects everything and everyone. One does not have to travel to a specific location to receive specific information from the field. The entire field is at all points in the universe at all times. This means that anytime or anywhere, you are always connected to all of the information in the universe.

Most psychic phenomena can be better understood utilizing this concept of a universal field of information. Because the field is everywhere at all times, any change in the field instantly influences the entire universe. This explains nonlocal influences, or action-at-a-distance, as I discuss in the Introduction. Some people are more skilled than others at focusing their connection to this information field; they are said to have psychic, telepathic or telekinetic capabilities. That is, reading information obtained nonlocally from the field is often labeled as paranormal. But the key word in the phrase "more skilled" is "more." We all possess these capacities, which can be developed further with practice.

I am fortunate to have been given the natural talent of being able to easily and selectively access intuitive information from the field. This includes the information in this book about the origin of the universe. It includes the ability to view the hologram—the three-dimensional projection containing all the information of a person—either locally or at a distance and thus facilitate healing. These are examples of intuitive perception that I am tuned to in my everyday life. Other abilities such as telepathy, clairvoyance, remote viewing and telekinesis seem to be part of or related to the same gift of being able to easily access the field. These abilities sometimes are referred to as a sixth sense.

Telepathy is the process of using mental images for communication rather than more commonly accepted means, such as writing and speaking. When both the sender and receiver are proficient at it, telepathy is an extremely efficient way to exchange information. Every one of us has the ability to communicate in this way, and it can be practiced just like any other skill. For people who have never tried this form of communication, it will seem like a huge challenge, similar to attempting to speak for the first time as an adult: One would not even have developed the facial muscles to enunciate words. Yet, with strong intention and focused practice, we can all become more aware of our ability to communicate telepathically.

Telepathy and healing operate essentially by the same mechanism. Healing is simply a focused, intentional kind of telepathy. In other words, telepathy in general is the mental transfer of various types of information, whereas healing is the transfer of information with the intent of influencing a person's health.

I have learned that there are two types of telepathy: local and nonlocal. Local telepathy involves sending and receiving mental images during a face-to-face conversation. Light emitted from one person influences the other person. Local telepathy (see Illustration 4) works via the field and also by an exchange of light locally, whereas nonlocal telepathy occurs solely by influencing the field of information. Light would not be able to efficiently carry information from one person to another over great distances without the field. When telepathically communicating with someone who is geographically distant, it is necessary to pick up and receive the images through your connection with the field.

I have occasionally met people with whom I can engage in a telepathic conversation. For instance, I communicated telepathically with a shaman at a Native American healing gathering in which I was participating. If another person and I are particularly aligned—that is, if the light frequency we emit is similar—then information can be transferred back and forth easily. I have found that when speaking aloud afterward, speech seems a crude form of communication and an awkward means of exchanging information in comparison to telepathic imaging.

Telepathic communication is not limited to people with similar light frequencies. It is happening all the time on a subconscious level, whether you are emitting a frequency similar to the other person's or not. But on a conscious level, telepathic communication can be more difficult between different frequencies. With practice, all of us can improve our telepathic communication skills by paying attention to our subtle feelings and thoughts.

Clairvoyance is the ability to perceive things beyond the usual five senses of sight, hearing, taste, smell and touch. We have all heard of detective mysteries that are solved through the information provided by a psychic. The clairvoyant is proficient at connecting information in the field to the crime. Some clairvoyants access this connection through a piece of the victim's clothing. Others connect through names, locations, voices or photographs. Each psychic has his or her own way of working. The striking commonality is that a point of reference, or intersection of the information, must occur between the psychic and an object with which the victim had some attachment. This is how information becomes forever entangled from this meeting point on.

Remote viewing is the ability to "see" images or events in another geographical location by going beyond our everyday perceptual means and accessing the field. An example of remote viewing is observing a distant scene during an out-of-body experience. I have remotely viewed my dad's office during an out-of-body experience and correctly identified items in the room. I have also experimented several times with reading street signs remotely, with some success.

When I was fifteen, I tried to remote view my uncle's house. I found myself in an out-of-body experience and in the area of my uncle's house. While trying to figure out exactly where I was, I looked at a street sign. It said "Empire Street"—not a road that I knew. When I looked at a map of the area, I learned that Empire Street is a couple of blocks from my uncle's house. I tried to remote view his house again and eventually found it. I believe remote viewing, like telepathy and clairvoyance, is a skill that can be developed by any one of us.

Telekinesis is the ability to move objects by mental means instead of physical means. When this has happened around me, it has been without any conscious plan on my part. In high school, my pen flew out of my hand many times. This occurred primarily when I was daydreaming and had no particular thoughts at all in my mind. On another occasion, I reached out to grab a nasal spray container. Just before I touched it, it launched into the air and hit the ceiling with great force. My dad, who was in the room with me, was shocked.

Some people are able to influence the physical realm remotely through intention. They can access information about an object from the field and modify that object's properties. For instance, Uri Geller, possibly one of the world's most famous psychics, bends spoons this way.

Accessing the field, especially nonlocally, also explains how distant healing works. The intention of one person affects the field locally, which then influences the other person nonlocally via the field. The field amplifies our every intent and influences changes accordingly, far beyond our conscious awareness.

When healing a person at a distance, I request a color photo-graph of that person's face. From the photo, I project the person's hologram in front of me. I don't understand exactly how this happens, but I instantly receive information on the person's health in the form of holograms, which appear before me.

To facilitate healing, I energetically alter the flow of energy to its optimal state, while paying special attention to areas where the energy appears stagnant, blocked or unusual. I describe to the person the problem areas as they appear to me. What I see depends on the subset of the person's internal information that I am exploring in the hologram. For example, if someone has chronic back pain, I would access the skeletal view of that person's health information. This view allows me to see where the pain originates. I am also able to get more detailed information at a cellular level should this be needed. With the information, I am then able to manipulate through my healing intentions the energy needed for that person's health to change. I mentally adjust the energy to its maximum potential for healing by removing energy blockages. The energetic change instanta-neously influences that person's hologram, which in turn registers in that person's body.

How long the energy takes to adjust depends on the person and the ailment; it could be hours, days, weeks or even months. I get some sense at the time of treatment of how efficiently the person has received the new information, and it varies greatly. With some people, it appears to me, when I see how they react energetically to a treatment, that they have made the energetic shift, yet almost immediately they revert to their original health pattern. Their health challenge just bounces back. Changes sometimes seem to be very elastic, which is evident to me when I see their hologram again, perhaps for another treatment. They have energetically reverted to the energy pattern of their original health problem. This tells me that changes will likely not be lasting or permanent.

The results that I get from my healings are directly related to the receptivity of the healee. This is why it is so important to review our openness to our energy and its healing possibilities. There are several possible reasons for achieving limited results in certain situations. We can be interfering in our healing potential by having self-limiting beliefs. Take the game of catch, for instance. Throwing the ball accurately is only half the game. To have a game going at all, the recipient or catcher must do his or her part. All the best throws in the world won't lead to a game unless someone is there willing and able to catch the ball. Likewise, you must be receptive in order for energy healing to work. It is important to accept and know that energy healing will work. My hope is that by explaining the science behind energy healing, you are able to better understand it and work with it. Don't be afraid to catch the ball: You are in the game, whether you think you are or not. Learn how to be the most effective player you can be.

We may not always be consciously aware of what our beliefs are. If our conscious intent is not synchronized with our subconscious ideas, then we are sending mixed signals into the field. We ourselves must be clear about what we want and expect from an energy healing. Some people are very well read on energy healing and yet they still may be inflexible in accepting healing information that may help their situation. Embracing the new means embracing change. This may be the most difficult requirement of all, as change is often unsettling. It is important to sometimes approach something new by knowing nothing, yet feeling everything. That is, the paradigms that we have all learned through academia and life experience play a major role in what we can and can't accept; when we are able to truly let go of the conscious restraints that we place on ourselves, we will react to our gut feeling.

There are a small number of people I've treated with whom I believe I do have an energetic connection, yet it doesn't seem to be an effective one. Perhaps our frequencies are not working together coherently. Or perhaps there are conflicting energies, similar to when an energy wave and an inverse energy wave meet and cancel each other out, with a resulting nil effect. This is not because of any conscious effort on the part of the healer or healee, but nevertheless it does effectively block any energy healing attempts. I hope in the future to have a better understanding of this so I may be able to connect more effectively in such situations.

In energy healing, as in life in general, the bottom line is attitude. Our attitudes stem from our beliefs. They guide us forward or backward depending on how we shape our reality: It is all a matter of one's perspective. The field responds to our every intention if we make it clear what that is. Ancient prophets and mystics were well aware of our connection to everything and the flow of nonlocal information that goes hand in hand with one's perspective. In many societies, the ruler—whether king or queen, emperor or empress, or chief— never made major decisions without consulting his or her prophets. Western cultures, in general, have lost respect for this way of knowing.

Many non-Western cultures are much more accepting than Western culture is of what exists beyond our five senses. Views within Western culture have become narrow and intolerant. We can readily accept that dogs can hear frequencies beyond our range, yet if humans hear anything that is beyond typical sensitivity, they are labeled odd or different. The same attitude prevails for unusual perception with any of the other four senses. Yet, all other animals rely heavily on the information they receive from the field. Many events occur in nature in which survival depends on accurately interpreting extrasensory information.

It seems to me that all of these psychic abilities—telepathy, clairvoyance, remote viewing, telekinesis and distant healing— are interlinked and interrelated. They all involve accessing the field of information for answers. If answers seem to come more easily for some, it is because those people are more focused when they ask a question. The field responds to what is asked of it.

You can influence greater change with your intentions by understanding how to clearly focus them in order to affect events. It is also possible to connect to more information by becoming aware of how you are habitually filtering the information which is continually running through you. By intentionally altering your filtering processes, you allow yourself to get in touch with more information vital to your well-being. These concepts are discussed in more detail in Chapters 6 and 7.

Our sixth sense—intuition—is similar to the other five senses in that we can fine-tune and sharpen it. Imagine someone who has never paid any attention to artwork critiquing a painting. Then imagine an artist evaluating the same painting. Who would have the most comprehensive perception of the painting? The artist. The master artist has developed his or her ability to see form and color. The sense of hearing works the same way. If you need a critical analysis of a symphony, a professional musician would be the best person to make an informed critique. Of course, the critique would be based on an existing knowledge base. The disciplined development of any of our five senses takes dedication and practice; our sixth sense is no different.

You can exercise your connection to frequencies from the field just like exercising a muscle. The more you exercise and use it on a regular basis, the more efficiently you can tune in to it. You can practice by paying more attention to your intuition, or gut instinct. When you feel very strongly about something, trust these feelings and act upon them.

Artists do not achieve mastery overnight. Some may become aware of their talents at a young age, long before they begin formal study. Most musicians in a symphony orchestra, even though talented, must spend years studying and practicing to qualify for the job. One needs passion and perseverance for the development of any talent. At the same time, anyone can enjoy art or music, whether exceptionally talented or not. Self-realization is about making the most of our own special gifts and fully appreciating the special gifts of others.

Through examining your belief systems (a topic I elaborate on in Chapter 7), you can learn to have better control of the flow of data from the field to you. This is the essence of self-empowerment. Ultimately, your thoughts and actions are your responsibility. We all have the ability through intention to project this energy from the field into our physical world. Your thoughts can and do influence your reality. You are always an active participant in the universal reality.

The field of information extends to all inanimate objects as well. For instance, I always insist that water be present during my workshops. With the positive healing intentions of the five hundred people present, the energy in the room is powerful. I can feel that the energetic properties of the water are intensified. This is how I know that water is affected by the intentions, thoughts and feelings it is exposed to. In a dominolike effect, thoughts affect you and everyone around you, as well as the air and water near you. We are surrounded by lakes, rivers and oceans; our atmosphere contains water; we ourselves are composed mostly of water. This is why the impact that good intentions have on water will be present all over our water abundant planet.

Is the field "out there" or within us, or both?

Both. The field is all places at all times. The entire field is at all points in space at all times.

How can I receive information from the field more easily?
Is there any way to strengthen my connection to it?

The best way to get information more easily is to understand where you are picking up the information from—namely, the field. Just know that you are connecting to this source of information which is being funneled through you. If you accept that all of the information in the universe is running through you, it's then just a matter of using your intuition to choose which information is important to you and acting on it. Become aware of how you are habitually filtering the information that is continually running through you from the field. Pay attention to your hunches and act on them. The best way to strengthen your connection to the field is thinking of your intuition as a muscle. Exercise it until it's stronger.

Is just asking a question in your mind the way to ask a question of the field?

Yes. I like to clear my mind of all thoughts and then ask myself the question, and see what comes to my attention in this calm state of awareness.

Chapter 4

Symphony of Light

Every cell is influenced and directed by light.

—ADAM

At my workshops I often do aura readings on several participants. What I see varies from person to person, but in the vast
majority of readings, what I see strongly correlates with the
physical ailment that the person is already aware of. For example,
in the auras of people with sciatic nerve problems, there are
defined distortions over the sciatic nerve. I can see a jagged
glowing or throbbing of light at the source of the pain. The pain
radiates along the nerve pathway, sending the person's back into
spasms. If I go in and do an energy treatment holographically, I
see this light gradually dim in its intensity and become smoother
as it sets into its new pattern of harmonious flow.

AURAS

The flow of energy in a harmonious pattern of light emissions is
the basis of all healthy life forms. Light coordinates all life
processes. Life is a veritable symphony of light.

Throughout history there have been people such as Edgar
Cayce who have been able to see the light that is emitted from all

forms of life; that is, the aura. Cayce (1877–1945) is best known as a psychic medical diagnostician and a reader of past lives. Many healers who can see or feel auras perceive a lot of information about the person whose aura they are viewing. The aura is subtle energy, a form of light at a particular frequency that is radiating from the living organism. Each of us radiates information through this aura. The harmonization of the light energy defines life itself, from the subatomic level to the cellular, to the whole organism and beyond. Subtle energy, the energy of life, is known by various names in different cultures. The Chinese refer to it as *qi* (pronounced "chi"), the Japanese as *ki* ("key"), and Hindus as *prana*.

Light is affected by illness—both disease and injury—as the body experiences change. Our bodies are constantly adjusting to differences, physical as well as psychological, in our well-being. I can see that through intentions we are consciously able to influence the light inside our bodies, which is in turn reflected and emitted outside of our bodies as an aura. Our bodies respond to every thought we think and every word we speak. We are directly affected physically by our feelings and intentions. Knowing this, each of us can maximize our well-being physically, emotionally and spiritually.

This light energy, or aura, connects us all to each other through information being communicated through it. Within our bodies, our cells use this vehicle of communication. By capitalizing on this concept, we are each empowered to re-create our optimal health. This, however, is just the beginning. Through this subtle energy we are all linked in a universal web of energy. Everything is just energy within a complex vibrating web. By helping ourselves through intention, we are positively influencing every other person and every other organism everywhere. Through manifesting our own empowerment, we naturally extend our awareness to a group consciousness, a global consciousness, and beyond these bounds to a universal consciousness. Thought has no boundaries.

Our thoughts and intentions create our reality by attracting what we are focusing on. Positive thoughts and expectations will bring positive results. For instance, I, like many athletes, practice positive thinking when I am weight training. When striving for a higher goal, such as benching a heavier weight or increasing the number of repetitions, I see the successful completion of the task in my mind's eye. The desired physical results are realized through intention of them. Of course, your goal must be a realistic one that you determine in increments. Expecting to win a marathon without adequate training is inconsistent with what your true expectations are. However, aiming to run five miles the first week, and ten miles the next week, increasing your endurance gradually, is a realistic goal. If you are already a marathon runner, wanting to better your race time is a realistic goal to work toward.

Learn ways to most efficiently access this ability to create your own reality that is within us all. Send yourself an intense message of what you want and focus on that. Be sure that your conscious thoughts are synchronized with your subconscious thoughts; this is analogous to making sure your goals are realistic. I explain this further in Chapter 5, on consciousness.

It is essential for people with health challenges to eliminate any underlying doubts or fears that they may feel about their way forward. Positive thoughts cannot be used to gloss over fundamental feelings of fear and negativity. Everyone's goal should be to replace nonconstructive thoughts and feelings with pure positive direction. Your body will reward you with a stronger immune system, more balanced emotions and a comforted spirit.

Every cell in the body responds to the subtle energy of light. Scientists typically view the body as a machine with biochemical reactions. In the future, science will verify what the ancient mystics knew: that energy is the most basic characteristic of life. These mystics had a deep understanding of many things for which there are no measuring instruments. Many of science's unknowns will be replaced by revolutionary knowns as measuring devices become more sophisticated. But whether humankind is capable of producing a machine sophisticated enough to measure the essence of life energy remains to be seen.

DNA is considered the basis of all life forms. It is responsible for the construction of our physical bodies and the replacement of cells as they become worn out. While DNA clearly is the blueprint of life for cellular reproduction, its information is dynamic, interactive and adaptable. Our DNA is not written in stone. I can see that our genetic makeup can be influenced through subtle energy. With every intention, you are emitting light that influences your DNA. Your intentions are constantly influencing your evolution.

In other words, thoughts and feelings can influence and reprogram our physical selves. By influencing our genetic codes, we are reprogramming its language and making adjustments to our holographic information. The people I have worked with on their healing journeys have taught me a great deal. In my first book, *DreamHealer,* I discussed the genetic holographic image, but I was uncertain as to how to work with it. I now have a much better understanding of it. As my learning has continued, I have had the opportunity to work with several people on their genetic disorders. I have learned that the information contained within DNA can be flexible. We can influence any aspect of ourselves.

Your genetic makeup influences how you react to your environment, but you still have a great deal of choice. DNA is dynamic and reacts to your environment. Intentions are part of that environment. This is the process that drives the evolution of all living organisms, including humans. For example, part of Nepal lies in the foothills of the Himalayas. One group of people who live there, the Sherpas, act as guides for the adventurers climbing Mount Everest. For many generations, these mountain dwellers have had to use oxygen more effectively in their bodies because of the high altitude where they live. Over time this trait has become engrained in the genetic makeup of the Sherpas.

How we react to our environment is dynamic. Our pattern of wellness, which is reflected in our energy, is also dynamic. It is easy to enhance the connection that we have with our own energy.

ENERGY EXERCISES

The following exercises will help you develop your skills in feeling and seeing your own energy, and then bringing in universal energy to your body.

Feel Your Energy

1. Rub your palms together in a circular motion. Feel the generation of heat. This is your own energy.
2. Now hold your hands about two inches apart, palm to palm. Push your hands toward one another without actually moving them. That is, visualize your hands pushing toward one another. Feel the resistance, similar to two like magnets repelling each other.
3. Spread your hands varying distances apart and feel the same resistance.
4. Establish the threshold distance at which your palms can be separated and you still feel your energy. With practice, you will be able to increase this distance as you become more sensitive to energy.

Illustration 5 depicts both the energy around your hands and the resistance you should feel when doing this exercise.

See Your Energy

1. Against a dark background, hold your hands in front of you with your fingertips pointing to the fingertips of the other hand, about two inches apart (see Illustration 6).
2. Move your fingers slowly up and down and in and out. Think about the energy flowing from one fingertip to the other. You will see a faint line of energy passing between them. At first this may appear as a hazy band.

Practice this exercise against backgrounds of various colors. With practice, the energy flow will look more defined.

Bring in Universal Energy

1. Imagine all the energy of the universe circling above your head, available for your use (see Illustration 7).
2. Bring in energy through the top of your head and collect it in your heart area.
3. Send the energy from the heart area down through your right arm, through your right fingertips, back into your left fingers and up through your left arm and to the heart.
4. Continue to imagine this flow as an energy circuit: from your heart to right arm, right hand, right fingertips, to left fingertips, left arm and then to the heart.

At first you may see just a faint line. You will be surprised at how quickly, with practice, you will see defined energy flow.

How to See a Person's Aura

Look past the person whose aura you want to see. Concentrate on an area about two inches above the shoulders or head (see Illustration 8).

At first you may see a slight shimmering aura, similar to the one shown in Illustration 9. The aura may appear as a subtle emanation surrounding material objects. Some people describe this as similar to heat waves, others as a misty fog. It will likely be far easier to see the aura after you've done a treatment using the visualizations discussed in Part 3 of this book. Few people will see the aura with the color intensity shown in Illustration 10, but with practice, you may see the defined flowing colors. Keep practicing!

How to See the Flow of Energy

A body without injury or illness would have harmonious energy flow. A body developing an injury or illness has energy that is beginning to lose its path or direction. A body with a fully developed injury or illness has a break in the energy flow, as depicted in Illustration 11, and can't find its way back to a harmonious energy flow, or wellness. Here is an advanced exercise to see energy flow; keep it in mind as a long-term goal.

1. Stand in front of a full-length mirror.
2. Relax your eyes by not focusing on anything.
3. Practice seeing and feeling your own energy flow.

Try doing this in both light and dark conditions. You can do this exercise with another person as well, practicing to see each other's energy flow. At first, you may be guided primarily by intuition—by feeling the energy. Soon you will be able to see it as well. As you develop this skill, you will find that your intuitive sense increases along with your healing ability. Trust that you can do this.

Everything that we tell our bodies through thoughts, words, emotions and beliefs is communicated through subtle energy, that is, through various frequencies of light. Subtle energies have a wide range of frequencies. Effectively connecting to this energy is a skill each of us can master by developing our inner processes of feeling, "seeing" and knowing. It is up to each of us to recognize this communication skill that we can consciously access. Intention is the most powerful tool for this process. We must get in touch with our own awareness.

Reading Auras

As I mentioned earlier, usually at my workshops I call upon several volunteers and read their auras. What shows up in the auras is more than an indication of what is happening physically. The aura reflects a variety of information, ranging from the emotional makeup of the person to his or her thoughts and intentions. With all the movement of energy in the aura, it is generally not possible to pinpoint the exact location of the physical ailment, but it is possible to determine the general area of the problem.

Each illness looks slightly different in the aura. As well, every aura has many variations, suggestive of minor blockages or potential difficulties. So my challenge when reading an aura is not so much to find physical problems but to sort through all the blockages and potential problems and select the one that is likely to be bothering the person most.

Certain ailments have definite signatures on the aura. Problems with the sciatic nerve are generally easy to see, as they look almost the same on everyone. When an aura has a static look, similar to a blurry television screen, this generally indicates that there is a problem with the nerves, emotions or skin.

Anyone can practice reading auras by looking at an aura in a dark room. Many people will see what looks like distortions over certain areas of the person's body. These distortions will likely appear over a region that is bothering the person. However, do not be discouraged if the person cannot make sense of what you relate: The aura shows a variety of factors, including old problems, emotional problems and developing problems. Medications tend to add a cloudiness, making it much more difficult to read the aura. Do not strain your eyes looking at a specific area on the person. Scan the entire body and pay attention to the information that comes to you. Practice this, and you will be surprised at how accurate you become.

Another point to keep in mind when reading someone's aura is that pain felt in one location does not necessarily mean this is where the source of the problem is. You might pick up on an area that seems unrelated to where the person experiences the pain, but they may in fact be closely linked.

If you are not seeing anything at all when trying to read someone's aura, practice relaxing and using your intuition. Ask yourself, what is wrong with this person? and the first thing that pops into your head may be significant. This nonanalytical approach allows you to practice the development of your intuition.

The following Advanced Aura Reading Exercise will be difficult to master, and you might want to first practice the exercise on page 50, How to See a Person's Aura. This is an advanced exercise because it requires integrating left-brain activities, or logical thinking, with the holistic view of the right brain. You must be open-minded and try it without hesitation. The only thing holding you back is your own mind. Just relax and feel it. This exercise will help you trust your intuition. Once you master the skill of combining your left- and right-brain activities, it becomes easy.

Advanced Aura Reading Exercise

1. Visualize energy extensions coming out of your fingertips, similar to claws or chopsticks.

2. Put your hands several inches above the person's body and physically comb the aura with your fingers, letting the energetic extensions of your fingertips penetrate deep into the person's body.

3. Run your hands along the aura very slowly and smoothly until you feel a dull pain, a sensation in your fingertips or a slight resistance similar to two like magnets repelling each other. At this point there is an energy blockage, which likely indicates a physical ailment of some sort.

4. Once you have identified the location of the blockage on the aura, attempt to remove the blockage. This is the difficult part.

5. You must keep pinching the blockage and pulling it away from the aura. Do not worry about these blockages affecting your health; they will not affect you if your intention is to not be affected by them. If you are worrying about this, then you likely have some subconscious intent to pull the energy blockage into yourself. Do not worry about it and nothing negative will happen. No negative outcome will occur when your intent is positive.

Moving your hands will help you in your visualization of removing the energy blockage. In your mind's eye, picture grabbing onto a problem in the aura and throwing it away. Simultaneously, physically move your hands on the person's aura. The aura will be physically influenced by your hand movements.

6. Dispose of the energy blockages by throwing them into the garbage, a vacuum or a black hole. Let your imagination dictate this. The energy of problems will dissipate without a host organism.

Combing Your Energy

Use this technique to give yourself a massage of light energy. Visualize light emitting from your fingertips as pure white light of pure intentions (see Illustration 12). Usually it can first be seen as smokelike extensions from the fingertips or faint shimmering lines. Some people report seeing small bolts of lightning. Relax and let it flow.

1. Imagine that your energy fingertips are like a comb. Sometimes your energy, like your hair, gets knots and tangles in it. Use your energy fingernails to comb out these knots so that your energy flows smoothly again.

2. Start at the top of your head and "comb down" over your entire body, about two inches out from your body. No actual physical contact is necessary. Feel and see the energy. It now flows smoothly and effortlessly in a harmonious pattern.

3. Comb the energy down to your feet and out through your soles. Many people feel an immediate calming sensation when doing this.

It may be easier for you to feel rather than think about what is happening, making energy healing a more realistic experience for you. Try changing the colors of light emanating from your fingertips and feeling the variations. You will know what suits you best when you find what color (frequency) you resonate with most effectively: You will feel sensations such as tingling or heat. Always be ready and willing to alter your visualizations and techniques. Only you can assess what works best for you. Know that you are doing these techniques correctly and that you are on the right path.

You can comb someone else's energy as well as your own using this technique.

Children usually feel an intense calming immediately; I find it to be especially effective with hyperactive children. Pets love it, too.

I believe everyone has the ability to heal themselves and others. This is built into our physical, emotional and spiritual natures as human beings. Some people are born with more innate readiness to use this ability than others. As with any talent, the time it takes each person to master reading auras will vary. Ultimately, it is a matter of motivation and practice.

In the realm of subtle energies, it is difficult to translate into words what is more of a nonverbal knowing. As you become more familiar with these exercises and skills you will become more familiar with trusting your feelings and your sense of knowing.

I have learned so much from working with many people who understand the power we all have to re-create our own health. Everything can be positively adjusted as we become tuned to the power of thought. I hope to be able to use this information to help others in many types of situations. One of my goals is to set up teaching centers so I can teach people some of my techniques. There are no bounds to what we can achieve in the re-creation of ourselves.

BIOPHOTONS

Biophoton emission is the scientific term for the communication and flow of subtle energy and information in the form of light between living cells and organisms. I offer the following brief scientific overview of biophoton emissions for those interested in the technical aspect. In your own healing, it is necessary to know only what you are going to change and how you plan to go about it. However, the science behind understanding healing may help some people put together the pieces of the puzzle.

Every time a chemical bond forms, light is absorbed in that bond (see Illustration 13). Every time a chemical bond breaks, light is emitted (see Illustration 14). At any given point in your body, there are trillions of chemical bonds forming and breaking; therefore, light is constantly being absorbed and emitted in your body. This light plays an essential role in catalyzing or inhibiting various chemical reactions throughout the body.

Every chemical bond that forms has an ideal frequency for that specific bond. In order for that bond to take place, the surrounding light must alter its frequency to be more aligned with the ideal frequency for that bond formation. The closer the light is to the optimal frequency range, the more easily the chemical reaction will occur. For small molecules, the influence that light has on the reaction rate is immeasurable, but for large molecules such as proteins and DNA, these varying light frequencies have a great influence on the rate of reaction.

Everything emits its own energy signature. Every living thing coordinates all of its life functions through its unique pattern of energy frequencies. With every intention there are countless neurons sending pulses of energy to other neurons. Whenever a neuron sends an impulse to another neuron, there is a charge buildup between membranes. A spark then transfers the charge between the neurons, creating an impulse. This spark is quite visible, as it emits large amounts of light, which permeates the entire body, catalyzing and inhibiting various chemical reactions throughout the body. This is how and why I see thought patterns as light.

Every illness emits a signature frequency of light. The body recognizes this information and intensifies its immune reaction accordingly. This emitted light is visible to me: I see what "signature frequencies" for diseases. For example, when asthma in someone, it has the appearance of a thick foggy substance in the airways of the lungs. Every cell within the lungs appears contracted. As I'm doing the treatment, I see the fog dissipate. I ask the person I'm treating to imagine burning the blockages out at the same time, until I see the air passages clear.

Some diseases, specifically some types of cancer, inhibit the release of light, so the body doesn't readily recognize the illness as being a problem. Our body's biochemical responses are initiated by the body's response to biophoton emissions; if this is blocked through the cloaking ability of the cancer, the disease remains invisible to the body's immune system, and it can grow unde-tected for some time. However, the light will intensify as the disease progresses, until the body becomes aware of its presence and responds. I have had some experience with this invisibility mechanism of cancer. Very rarely, I can't "see" cancer, but it shows on a scan. It is important to know that through the intention of the person, the immune process can still be stimulated. That is, the fact that a disease is cloaking the light energy does not mean that the body does not have a functioning immune system.

Energy treatments make use of the frequency signature, or wave, of disease. When I do a treatment, I reach a coherent resonance with the person's frequency and emit a wave inverse to that which the illness is emitting. This inverse energy wave neutralizes the frequency the disease is emitting. The person's body receives the signal, resonates with this new frequency and absorbs this energy as information. It then registers how to neutralize the problem and sets healing into motion. The basis of everything I see in holographic healing is light. Biophotons emitted from every process in every cell is the light that I see when I am doing a treatment.

Light can also help speed up chemical reactions in the body. Let's say I have a problem with my foot which I intend to heal. My healing intention simultaneously releases light and biochemicals. Light travels faster than biochemicals and so reaches my foot first and prepares foot cells to receive the body's biochemicals necessary to initiate the healing process. By the time the biochemicals physically attach to the cell, the cell is ready and waiting: All the biochemicals are aligned so that the process occurs efficiently. Although this chemical reaction may have a relatively small effect, cumulatively, these light emissions have a large effect on the organism.

The cumulative light frequencies emitted from a multi-cellular organism coordinate and unify all of the cells into one harmonious organism. Light coordinates life.

Remember, light from one organism (person) is capable of entering other organisms and influencing it. This is how your healing thoughts and intentions affect those around you. The light emitted from your intentions enters another person, influencing a series of chemical reactions that benefit the person's health.

For this reason, it is essential that you change not only your own intentions to be more aligned with healing but encourage those around you to be positive as well. If you are positive and everyone around you is negative, the light emitted from negative energy counters what you are trying to do. Likewise, if everyone around you is positive, their intentions will amplify your intentions.

Every thought you think influences light, which influences those around you, which influences life. That is why it is essential to reprogram your thought patterns in the direction of habitual positive thinking since it truly does make a difference.

I find it interesting that I can see by looking at someone's aura and looking at them holographically how light emissions are affected by drugs. This is because drugs—of any type—alter the biophoton emissions that are emitted by the body. When I look at someone who is on toxic chemotherapy, my vision is completely obscured, as though layers of clouds are blocking my view. Even over-the-counter medications change body chemistry and alter my ability to see clearly what is happening in the person's body. The good news is that even if you are taking medication, you are able to assist your own healing through your intention, which is your most powerful ally.

Distant healing and healing face-to-face both involve light emissions. Light emitted from a person's intentions does not travel by ordinary means. Rather, the connection works in a complex manner by influencing the field of information that we all share. The action is instantaneous and does not "travel" within the intervening space (see Illustration 15).

Since becoming a college student, I have been working primarily on short-term cases. Pain is usually remedied quickly with just a few treatments. For example, a fellow with a broken finger contacted me. He was in his first semester at university and had already missed ten days of school when we connected. The orthopedic surgeon used a pin to set his finger but in doing so inadvertently bent the nerve around the pin. The pinched nerve was causing the student excruciating pain. The doctor, unaware of the problem, prescribed high doses of painkillers, which made him too lethargic to attend classes.

When I looked at the student, which I did through a photo-graph, since we live 1000 miles apart, I could see that his nerve was pinched from the setting pin. The nerve appeared to me as white light, and I could see it pulsating. Pulsating white light is indicative of a throbbing pain. I could see that the white light of the nerve was bypassing an area near the pin. Through my intentions, I used energy to reroute the nerve. After one treat-ment, the student was pain-free, and once he cleared his system of the painkillers, he returned to his classes.

Modern medicine does not yet have the technology to examine nerves in such detail as this situation required. I can go in and holographically see the nervous system. It is obvious where the problem is because I energetically see the pain as it ripples out from the source. Or, in the case of the student with the broken finger, I was able to calm the nerve and reset it into a new position. The student felt my treatment; he described it as "all tingly"—as though he were placing his hand near a sparkler. He reported falling asleep immediately after the treatment, even though he hadn't taken any painkillers, and he felt fine the next morning, still without having taken any drugs.

ELECTROMAGNETIC FREQUENCY INTERFERENCE

Recently, I had a very interesting experience with auras and electromagnetic frequencies. While I was visiting the Institute of Noetic Sciences (IONS) campus in Petaluma, California, Dr. Dean Radin, the institute's chief scientist, gave me a tour of the research facilities. What interested me most was a Faraday cage the institute had built for psychic research. Named after its inventor, physicist Michael Faraday, the Faraday cage was first built in 1836. It is designed to prevent the passage of electromagnetic waves through a type of shielding. Because there are no electromagnetic waves, and therefore no electric field inside it, it was useful in conducting electrical studies. Although it was not designed for the paranormal research it is used for at IONS today, it is proving very useful in that field.

My parents and I walked into this room with Dr. Radin and the door was closed behind us. It was amazing. I saw for the first time what an aura looks like when it is not being bombarded with unwanted electromagnetic frequencies. The auras looked clean, without any jagged edges or static-looking texture. All auras that I had seen up to this point looked frazzled. I was unaware of this constant impact of EMF, or electromagnetic frequency, which is the magnetic energy that is all around us. This was an unexpected revelation. Since I had never had the opportunity to see auras in this pristine form, I had no expectation of what they should look like. I am excited about the possibilities that the Faraday cage presents, and in the future, I hope to test the effectiveness of healing from within a Faraday cage. For instance, I wonder if a face-to-face treatment would be more effective in the cage, as the auras are so much clearer to me. Also, I wonder whether this clearness of aura would affect the efficacy of distant healing.

From this experience, it is clear to me what an enormous impact EMF has on our health and wellness. Several years ago, I underwent a brain-mapping test. I was curious to see if my brain wave activity changes when I access someone's hologram for healing. A cap placed on my head was wired with electrodes to measure brain activity as I connected to someone's hologram. It seemed like a wonderful idea until the mild electrical current, the electromagnetic field, was turned on. Immediately I felt uncomfortable and distressed. There was no way I could connect to anything or anyone in my agitated state. I also immediately got a headache and could not concentrate. The test was over none too soon. I had been unable to do anything during the entire test because of the pain and distress I felt. The headache stayed with me for the afternoon.

My physical reaction to the electrical current surprised me. The only conclusion I could reach is that I am sensitive even to very low voltage being applied to my head. I was concerned that it might have damaged some of my connection to the field, but the negative effects were temporary.

I have noticed that I don't feel well if I am near high-voltage power lines for any length of time. Also, I am always aware of my cell phone because I feel numbness in my body where I carry it. I believe that we all are affected by a variety of electrical currents that surround us in modern life. Apparently, I am just more sensitive than the average person to the effects of electromagnetic frequency.

Generally, the level of electromagnetic frequency interference that we are usually exposed to does not appear to be a major problem when I do aura readings. We have all grown accustomed to their existence. Electromagnetic frequencies certainly do have an effect on auras and may aid in the effectiveness of healing as well. I look forward to exploring that comparison some day.

When did you first see auras?

I have always been able to see auras, the swirling glow of varying colors around living things. When I was young, I knew that people on television were different from people I see in person because I was not able to see the auras of people on the television screen. Whenever we went for a drive, I was always the first one to spot animals in the bushes or on the roadside because it was their auras I saw.

Is the aura one of the various holographic views of a person?

The aura is not a holographic view. Rather, an aura is the light emitted from a person's body, which extends beyond the physical self.

Do plants have auras, and if so, how do they appear to you?

Yes, all plants have a colorless aura. This energy which surrounds them may appear as a shimmering clear aura. Intuitively, I know that this is because they lack the intense emotions that all animals possess. This is not to say that they do not have emotions but that they are unable to experience the range of emotions that the animal world can.

Is energy influenced by thought?

Yes, energy is influenced by thought, since thought is a form of energy. I am able to see that every thought is initiated by light and immediately followed by biochemical reactions. When you have a thought, neurons are fired and light is thus emitted. Many things are influenced by thoughts. At the quantum level, quantum particles are being influenced by thoughts. Our thoughts influence things on the microscopic level and radiate to the macroscopic level, far beyond our conscious awareness.

You say that the harmonization of light defines life itself. Would you elaborate on this?

Basically, light emissions synchronize life itself. This synchronization of light is what keeps life organized. In a multi-cellular organism, all the cells are working together by synchronized light emissions. Any multi-cellular organism, even a single cell organism, depends on light to keep things functioning in a harmonious way, to keep everything coordinated.

What role does genetic predisposition play in a person developing a disease?

If you have a genetic predisposition to a disorder, you try to avoid the risk factors that increase the possibility of its manifestation. However, your thoughts and intentions play a significant role in whether the disorder is triggered. If you are worried about the probability of getting this illness, you are not intending it to manifest, but your thinking about it might have the same result. DNA is sensitive to light and DNA will react to light quickly (see Illustration 16), so the light emitted from your intentions will have an effect. If you are thinking about it constantly, the light emitted from those thoughts will increase the probability that you will manifest the problem or get that illness. DNA is dynamic.

PART 2

What We Make of Life

Chapter 5

Consciousness

Our consciousness, as energy, appears to generate spontaneous "thought links" to the field.

—ADAM

$\mathcal{A}$fter my vision of the bird, any time a question popped into my head, I was bombarded with vast amounts of information that addressed it. Naturally, I had many questions about consciousness, especially how it relates to our health and healing. Each of us in our role as an observer creates our own reality. It follows that our own health and healing is part of this observation. Our individual consciousness is how we relate to every experience. By understanding more about the nature of consciousness, we will be better equipped to answer such questions as, what is my role in the universe? and, how can I create my new healing reality? By accessing the field beyond space and time, we are all able to influence our own health accordingly through our intentions.

The web of interconnectivity—the field of information— contains every possible event, past, present and future. From these potential events, the observer creates his or her reality. Each of us creates an order or pattern through the act of observing. Our thoughts, words and actions are expressions of what we perceive as our reality. Our reality is completely subjective. Objectivity is impossible, since simply by the act of observing an event we have an influence on it. There is no way we can understand or observe this theoretical objective reality in any way without making it subjective. To achieve pure objectivity we would have to be observing an event from outside our universe. Therefore, all of our perceptions are biased opinions—that is, subjective.

A person's pattern of observing things in life is a direct result of his or her life experiences. The way in which we individually filter information and process it for our own use is our individual consciousness. This is the foundation for our individuality, even though one's individual consciousness extends to everything that one connects to within the web.

The filters in our brains have been developed through all of our life experiences. For example, if we are distrustful of people as a result of past experiences, we will observe current events with mistrust and suspicion. At one of my workshops, I met a woman who said she was unable to form any relationships, either friendships or intimate relationships. She thought that everyone was "after something" and past experience taught her to trust no one. On the other hand, if we have found in the past that relationships are fulfilling to us, we will be more receptive to such incoming possibilities. (I discuss how we can change these filters for the betterment of our health in Chapter 6 in the section, Adjusting Your Attitude.)

Consciousness is everything we know to be real through our five senses and our intuitive sixth sense. Individual consciousness also can be thought of as the self-awareness connecting us to the universal field of collective consciousness. In this way, we are connected to everyone and everything in the universe. (I discuss collective consciousness in more detail later in this chapter.)

Which came first? The universe? The field? Or consciousness? We can only speculate. As I mention in Chapter 2, the first particle of matter was formed from fluctuations of energy. The field of information is the link between energy fluctuations, so it makes sense to say that the field preceded the Big Bang. It is possible that consciousness also existed before the Big Bang. If it did, it would not have been as complex as it is now, since it had no matter with which to form links. Consciousness would have merely existed as a probability in a sea of energy.

Is there a guide of some sort outside of us? Are our conscious thoughts guided by an external force? In theological terms, is there a god? What or who or even whether our thoughts are determined is certainly a subject for discussion (and I elaborate on it further in Chapter 7). Some would say that our self-reflective consciousness and search for meaning suggests the concept of a god. Many people refer to the collective consciousness of their particular religion, such as God, Allah or Jehovah, as the consciousness of everything in the universe influencing or interacting with everything else. According to

major religions, there was a consciousness that existed
before the Big Bang.

I will leave the theological debate to others. What I will
describe here is how I see brain neurons processing information.
The brain organizes information in a way that is manageable and
useful to the person. It does this by gathering informational
frequencies into a resonant form that we can make use of.
Subconscious thoughts are the result of spontaneous information that brain neurons pick up from the field. From this
random information, the brain assesses what is of importance
and sends this information to the conscious mind for action.

You are constantly receiving information from the universe.
The process is spontaneous, and your brain is constantly filtering this infinite amount of information that passes through
you. Your brain is a complex web of neurons with signals and
responses. How you interpret the incoming information is a
matter of your brain assessing what is important and what is
not. That decision relates to your life experiences: Your life
experiences determine what information is important to you
and what isn't.

The brain is the physical organ of the mind. The brain filters
information; the mind processes it. The individuality of the
mind lies in how a person is uniquely interpreting information
from the field that we are all receiving. Even if we all witnessed
the same event, each of our minds is interpreting it uniquely.
Each of us sees only what we expect to see based on past experi-

ences. The rest of the information that we receive will stay as a subconscious stream of unused background data.

Everyone picks up on different information at different times. The process is dynamic. What information the brain picks up and how it picks it up is constantly changing with our environment. For instance, if we are in a noisy, chaotic setting, we will find it impossible to focus on and process every action and sound. If we are in more subdued surroundings, it is easier to concentrate on one event at a time.

There are many frequency levels—or, one might say, levels of consciousness—even within the same person. Your brain is always sorting out these different frequencies. When you are sleeping, you are doing so at a particular frequency. When you are awake, you are functioning at another specific frequency. When you meditate, you are operating at yet another frequency. These various frequencies allow you to make connections to the universal energy field in various ways, but still within your own frequency spectrum. A good analogy is measurements. One might use various angles and lengths to describe an object. Alternatively, it could be characterized in terms of its weight or density. These are all expressions of the same object, and simply represent it in different ways. All these frequencies are vibrations at the subatomic level, and are part of a complex array of frequencies. Certain information is available at a particular frequency, and other information at another frequency. There is no hierarchy of vibrations—no higher or lower vibration—just *different* vibrations.

There are millions of neurons in our brains, each with its particular frequency that enables us to explore several thoughts simultaneously. If you have several neurons all at different frequencies then you are connected to several different sets of information simultaneously. It is therefore possible for your brain to process several thoughts at the same time. This ability to be multi-focal is essential in our fast-paced society. It is referred to as multi-tasking. When we are in an altered state of consciousness, such as a meditative state, more neurons are on the same frequency. That is what we seek to achieve in a calm, meditative state. This allows less interaction with incoming information.

We are capable of receiving enormous amounts of information, but we are limited in our capability to decode it. Imagine that, rather than focusing on the specific information that you usually process selectively as you need it, you are acutely aware of everything in your surrounding environment—every detail of every sight, sound, smell, taste and feeling being processed at the same time. Think about what that would really involve. At any point in time, we have a finite number of neurons in the brain available to decode this information, so we must have a selection process as to what we need. This is our consciousness.

Many of us think of consciousness as residing solely in the brain. However, every atom, every cell, every subatomic particle in the body has some form of consciousness as a result of connecting to the field. Each of our cells can react with its environment, and live or die independently of the body as a whole.

The cell makes all of these functional decisions through the use of its cellular memory. What was successful for it will be a repeated behavior, and what was unsuccessful will not be repeated.

The brain is capable of coordinating every cell in your body into a resonant frequency, organizing them so that they work together. When they are at a common energy frequency, you will be able to make a more effective connection to the field. As cells resonate together, this allows them to function as a whole entity, rather than as separate parts. If you are thinking about a past event, your brain is making a specific connection to the pattern of frequencies making up the memory of that event. The brain can sort out an enormous amount of data from the field and make it manageable so that we are not overwhelmed. It does this by organizing the incoming information into a pattern that we understand, and then signals the other cells accordingly.

To again use the analogy of a pond, the universal energy field is like one huge pond, with people the many ripples in that pond. Focal points of individual consciousness are the spots where the ripples originate. Every time you think a thought, the thought links to a piece of information. Think of it as the thought reaching out to grab a piece of information from a common field of consciousness—the pond. By grabbing this information, it affects something else (the piece of information) that is also in this field, causing a ripple in the pond. This ripple initiates a domino effect.

Think of each individual consciousness as a pebble. With every thought, your pebble (which represents your uniqueness) is being dropped into the pond. Each of your thoughts is represented by the same pebble. Another person's thoughts are a different pebble, which also causes a ripple when dropped into the pond. All the ripples in the pond interact. Everything makes a connection to everything else.

We are making connections all the time, whether we are aware of it or not. From our subjective point of view, we are each making unique connections according to our personalities and insights. Every experience in life is subjective, based on our perception of reality using our individual sensory input. From a scientific or objective perspective, our thoughts are all energy. So, while every living organism makes a unique connection to this field—that is, everything makes a connection through a different frequency—it is all the same energy.

After you die and go on to the next life (I discuss the concept of reincarnation in detail in Chapter 8), your energy, or essence, is the same pebble but in a different body. Your frequency patterns are the result of light emissions similar to those in your previous life. You are the same energy and the same vibrations; you simply reside in a different body. And while you are the same original conscious energy, this energy is constantly evolving. It does not change just when you die; it has been constantly changing since its origin. All matter continuously taps into this field and is constantly evolving.

If we can't make sense of the information we receive, it is possible that someone else may decode it for us. That is, their point of consciousness, or their brain, decodes the information, then their "ripple" in the pond interacts with our ripple. This is a natural process of information flow. We can pick up the information about any organic or inorganic thing in the universe—a bird, a plant, even a rock—because they are connected to the same field. It takes practice to do this. We are more complex than a rock because we are actively, dynamically and intentionally directing energy and thought patterns.

The flow of energy as information and our access to it are constantly evolving and changing. With continued evolution, we will all be able to access information from the field more easily. Our intuitive abilities increase as our skills to listen to them are developed. I call this tuning in. Most people have experienced this to some degree and know it as intuition. You are constantly receiving information subconsciously in the form of hunches, ideas or images. People who are visually oriented will tend to receive pictures; those who are more auditorily oriented may hear voices. The data you receive is not only from yourself and your own body but is information being emitted by others. In fact, all objects—animate and inanimate—emit information.

Tuning in to and deciphering this data is a survival mechanism. For example, you may get a feeling that you shouldn't eat something, and it turns out to be poisonous or that you are allergic to it. I always knew that I shouldn't eat kiwi fruit, yet I had never even tasted it. When I was about eight years old, my dad made a milkshake for my sister and me. He added kiwi without telling me, knowing I would refuse to taste the drink if I knew it contained kiwi. He thought my dislike of kiwi had no basis. Within a minute of swallowing the milkshake, my face became itchy and started to swell. Even as a small child, I had connected to the information that I shouldn't eat kiwi.

ALIGNING THE CONSCIOUS AND SUBCONSCIOUS MIND

As I mentioned earlier, it is important that your conscious and subconscious thoughts and intentions be synchronized. Make certain that when you consciously say, "I know that I can do it," this thought is in tune with the subconscious voice deep within you.

Synchronizing your conscious and subconscious thoughts is a skill that can be developed through practice. It is like playing the piano. Playing a tune with your dominant hand is pretty straightforward. Adding the accompaniment of the other hand seems almost impossible at first. You feel as though you need to keep track of two separate actions simultaneously. But with practice, coordination of both hands becomes second nature.

To synchronize your conscious and subconscious mind, you must become aware of your subconscious thoughts. One practice strategy is to quiet your mind. In the stillness, ask for information about subconscious blocks and wait quietly for answers.

Then consciously intend to let go of subconscious blockages. Do this regularly. Your goal of creating harmony within your intentions will make your visualizations more effective.

The game of golf is also a good example of coordinating conscious rational thoughts with intuitive knowledge. In golf, as in any sport, you must focus on numerous details while at the same time allowing yourself to just feel the connection that you are making to the game. As I watched golfers on the course, it looked like an easy game. How complicated could it possibly be to swing a club and hit a little white ball? During my first lesson, the pro had me grasp the club in a certain grip, stand at an exact distance from the ball, position my front foot precisely and then move the club behind me in a certain way while rotating in a specific motion. Now came the easy part, or so the pro said. I just had to relax and swing. What he was saying was, "You now have the information and the clear intention to hit the ball properly; just get out of the way and let your subconscious do the job."

THE UNCONSCIOUS STATE: COMA

I have been able to communicate with many people in comas, with some wonderful results. However, time is of the essence when working with those in comas. Immediately after the trauma, body memory in light emissions is still prominent. The biophoton emissions are evident to me, which makes stimulating them more straightforward. This light fades over time, making the reversal of the injury more difficult. When the biophoton emissions dim in intensity, it is as though memory fades. After this point, the person must relearn each forgotten skill, such as cognitive and communication abilities. The neural pathways (see Illustration 17) do not instantaneously transfer information as they did previously. As time passes, healing becomes more difficult, but it is still possible. Neural pathways can be regenerated but it takes energy and time.

In preparation for a treatment on someone in a coma, I ask the relatives to e-mail recent photographs of family and of happy events and gatherings. This is because the comatose person will recognize those in the photograph and will want to regain consciousness to join them. As well, any details about the accident are helpful, including the circumstances of the injury. With this information, I start to update the comatose person about what happened. This sometimes sparks the wake-up call.

A factor that I have noted when treating comatose people is that I can see that they receive the messages that I send without any judgment: They process it just like any other incoming information. I don't need to be concerned about their belief systems and past experiences interfering, as they are not actively filtering out what they think they don't need. The part of their brains that guide their awareness is not functioning properly. This part usually filters through all incoming information, streamlining what they think is needed for processing at any given time.

One teenager I worked with had survived a head-on car crash. She was unconscious and at first it was questionable whether she would live. Then her family faced another hurdle: They were told that if she lived she would have severe brain damage. Fortunately, her parents contacted me immediately after the accident. Her mother was active in the healing arts, and she understood what was involved in energy healing.

Although the daughter was comatose and couldn't verbally respond to me, she could understand when I sent information telepathically. I applied as much energy to her as possible through distant healing, concentrating on her brain and the intracranial bleeding caused by the impact. Energetically, I helped the girl stop the bleeding, and after several treatments, I could see that light was sparking along the neural pathways in her brain. It was apparent to me that she was coming out of her coma. The doctors told her parents that she would still have severe mental impairments, but I saw that she was going to be fine. Six months after the accident, the girl was attending university.

Another teenager's father got in touch with me immediately after she had fallen nearly sixty feet, hitting her head hard when she landed. Amazingly, the girl survived. However, she had extensive head injuries, and the doctors expected her to be severely brain damaged or even brain dead.

I started distant treatments on her right away, bringing into her brain and running through it as much energy as I could. I focused on stopping her intracranial bleeding and attempted to get the neurons sparking with light again. Her father was at her bedside during the first treatment. The girl was comatose and motionless. Immediately when the treatment began, her eyelids fluttered. This first movement since the accident demonstrated to him and to me that a significant connection to this healing had been achieved.

By the second treatment, I could see that there was some light activity in her brain, so I continued to bombard her brain with energy. It was clear to me that her neurons were regenerating and reactivating rapidly.

Doctors at the hospital left the family little hope for the girl's recovery. They reported that scans showed half of her brain to be dead. Paralysis to her left side seemed certain, and her right side was thought to be impaired as well. This was, of course, devastating news. But I did not agree with the doctors because what I saw energetically was increasing electrical activity in her brain. She was coming back.

After several treatments, I could see that the girl wanted to speak and was ready to do so with just a little energy stimulation. I focused on her speech during the treatment, and she began talking. Her first words were directed to her grandmother. She held her grandmother's arm and asked, "What happened to me?" It was no wonder she needed to ask this. It is exceptionally frustrating for injured people to find they are unable to communicate, especially at a time when they need to express their emotions about the traumatic event. It was a great relief for the girl to have this limitation removed from her life. She continued to improve as she regained both her mental faculties and physical movement. One month after the accident, she was sitting up in bed, eating, talking to visitors and going to physiotherapy. She had no paralysis.

It is encouraging to work with young people, as they have a powerful ability to regenerate after sustaining an injury. This is because of their youthful and strong physical selves, which are often accompanied by open-mindedness. One can often achieve results more quickly than when working with an older person.

Sometimes I can connect to the comatose person, but he or she is unable to return to a state of conscious awareness. I can only imagine what life is like from the perspective of people in comas. What we perceive as normal states of consciousness must seem so far removed from them. It seems as though they are in a very deep sleep, but unable to awaken from it.

I did a distant healing on a woman who was in a coma for five years following a car accident. Her infant son was unharmed in the accident. Her family was at her bedside when I did the treatment. I telepathically sent images of what had happened since the accident, as well as a current photo image of her son, which her family had sent me. As I sent her the images, tears started to roll down her cheeks. She understood, yet she just couldn't wake up.

A man had been in a coma for over thirty years after a car accident. Now age fifty, he had been nonresponsive since his late teens. From a distance of 2000 miles, I telepathically sent him images, and his family reported that he seemed to enjoy them: He smiled and appeared to be listening intently as if hearing music he liked. His father was thrilled when the man smiled directly at him. The man was unable to wake up into a conscious state, but that loving response was a heartwarming experience for his devoted family. His family also reported that during the treatment he moved more than he had ever done in the last thirty years.

I was contacted by the family of a man who fell into a coma during brain surgery. After six months in hospital, he still had not regained consciousness. I asked the family to be at his side during my treatment so they could report any changes during my distant healing. At the exact moment when I began the treatment, his eyes opened and he became conscious and responsive. He still wasn't able to see, as it had been so long since he had used his eye muscles. During this treatment, I sent into him as much energy as possible, and I could see sparking in his brain, as though the energy might be stimulating him. Sometimes it seems as though the treatment will produce results, but then the light fades or dissipates entirely soon after the treatment. Only in a subsequent treatment can I tell whether the brain has been activated enough to spark with light on its own.

The next evening I did another distant treatment, and I could see that the man was producing his own light in his brain. The family was once again at his side during the treatment, and they reported that this time he was able to see. The man has since attended one of my workshops, and his family is thrilled to have him back with them.

CONSCIOUSNESS OF ANIMALS

Some people have difficulty accepting that organisms other than humans have a consciousness. The idea that consciousness is something special, reserved only for humans, is quite arrogant. A great part of consciousness is perspective, and from an animal's perspective, the animal itself is more important than you or I.

Although I regularly read my cat's intentions telepathically, I never pick up any telepathic messages from her suggesting that she is searching for the deeper meaning of life, but this does not mean that she does not have consciousness. Consciousness is simply being aware of one's own presence. I am sure that my cat is well aware of hers. Just because she can't communicate in the same manner as a human doesn't mean that she is without conscious awareness.

All living creatures work within the same knowledge base and natural communication system as we do. Their cells communicate through subtle light energy just as ours do, and they are linked to all other animals and ourselves in the same way. Larger animals have more information than smaller ones because of their greater number of cells, which must be synchronized with the flow of data. The more highly evolved the animal, the more complicated the information is, since it contains both emotional and physical data.

Animals are acutely aware of information that they receive and process from the field. Their awareness is commonly referred to as instinct. Humans over time have learned to ignore most instinctual information and override it. We tend to concentrate instead on our conscious programming, which involves the societal concepts of time and space that we have learned about ourselves, our work and our relationships. Animals receive information from the field and act on it. What they process is pure, unadulterated guidance, free of the analytical clutter humans have. The field has always provided an organized flow of information to every organism.

Emergency workers who were first on the scene of the December 26, 2004, tsunami in Asia were amazed that no dolphins, whales or other sea life were washed up on shore. Many animals managed to escape this natural catastrophe because they can sense danger beyond the limitations of humans' five senses. It was reported that all of the elephant trainers were spared in this disaster because they were chasing their elephants as they ran to higher ground. Many people also were unwittingly saved as they ran after their dogs to higher ground. When an animal gets the danger signal, instinct takes over and all else is secondary; the fight or flight for survival takes precedence. Animals instinctively receive clear messages about what they need to do to preserve their lives, and they do not hesitate to act on it. This instinct is similar to the signaling that coordinates the movement of a school of fish when all the fish turn simultaneously and flee from danger. Every fish gets this signal at the same instant.

A disaster of the magnitude of the Asian tsunami radiates the intense energy of its danger signal over a great distance. The animal kingdom heeded the danger signal, which can be described as a collective consciousness resulting from this information resonating from the field. Those people in the vicinity who were sensitive to the disturbing energy patterns that radiate out from an earthquake must have experienced headaches, stomachaches or otherwise felt unwell. Yet, these feelings were likely dismissed because of the many obligations and distractions in their lives, as well as the social pressures that overrule these gut feelings.

You may know your own bodily signals better than you think. Everyone has a body area that pays the price when we feel tension. For some people, it is a pain in their neck. Others get stomach butterflies or migraines. Whatever the malady and wherever it strikes, we can learn to know our own signals. Listen to your inner voice, which takes the form of bodily signals. Then act on that information rather than overriding it.

Our connections to animals can be as meaningful as our connections to humans. Some time ago, a man sent me a photograph of one of his race horses. It had been ill and the veterinarian could not figure out why. Out of interest, because I have never connected energetically to a horse, I took a look at the photograph.

I could tell that the horse had eaten something that did not suit it because I saw excess light emanating from the stomach area. I also noticed that its upper back lit up as a problem area. I told the owner what I saw. He reported that some months earlier, the horse had injured its back while playing, and the problem in the stomach area could possibly be explained by a recent change in the horse's feed. The owner informed the veterinarian, and the horse was treated for these ailments. Shortly afterward, the horse owner e-mailed me to tell me that the horse was once again participating in equestrian competitions.

This demonstrated to me that connecting to animals, even nonlocally, is done in the same way as with humans. I was able to access the horse's hologram through a photograph just as easily as if it were a person, and its aura and light emission was no different.

COLLECTIVE CONSCIOUSNESS

Within the oneness of universal collective consciousness, each of us is unique. Although each of us has a distinctive energy frequency or vibration level, essentially, we are all one: a universal collective consciousness composed of the entire spectrum of frequencies. Every living organism (not just humans) is part of this. Everything, even inorganic material, is tied into a single conscious web of energy. However, nonliving substances are not as dynamic as living systems. Living organisms have a much more complex connection through the exchange of information.

This is because they are constantly at chemical disequilibria. This means that all biochemicals are constantly being adjusted and readjusted, which defines the dynamic processes of life itself. Only at death does a living organism reach a state of equilibrium.

It is possible for cells and complex organisms, such as people, to adjust to surrounding vibrations. This is essential in healing to get all of the cells working together. Each cell in our body has its own frequency. When all of our cells are working in unison, they collectively form a common frequency. During the group treatments at my workshops, after merging auras, a common frequency is reached among all participants: All frequencies are merged as one into a coherent pattern of energy resonance, and we all resonate at a common frequency. It is as if I am conducting an orchestra, creating harmony out of a chaos of musical notes. All of the individual holograms of information are merged into a collective hologram. The collective hologram functions as a group consciousness with healing intentions.

When I am doing a distant healing, I am aligning myself to another person's frequencies in order to make an intentional connection to the person's unique connection to the field. As I've mentioned, I do this through a photograph, which enables me to connect to the person's frequency and, from this, access the person's holographic record. When I focus my intention on a person at a distance, I connect to that person's hologram and decode it into useable information for health and healing, which allows me to change it and positively influence the person's health. By "decoding" I mean interpreting the information that I receive into an understandable form.

It is important to recognize that our consciousness extends beyond our individual selves to a collective consciousness, which links us to everything in the field. The more extensive the scope of this link, the more information is contained in the connection. It is like a camera being opened to a wider aperture. We get the broader prospective of the big picture, a more expansive focus.

When more conscious beings are connected to the same focused intention, a stronger and more intense bond is formed in our collective consciousness. This synchronicity of group consciousness can be strengthened by a common focus or intention. The wonderful possibilities that lie ahead will be chosen from all the positive outcomes imaginable. I believe that this is the same principle that will eventually help us realize a true global consciousness. Imagine the possibilities if millions of people in the world merged their auras as one. When we talk about the world reaching a higher level of conscious awareness, it is the result of many people merging their frequencies as one into a coherent pattern of resonating energy. Energy resonates as a singular unified conscious intention. The realization that we are all one will heal the world.

I believe that consciousness is becoming more complex all the time as the collective consciousness rapidly evolves to higher levels. People are becoming more aware of how consciousness functions and are making better use of it. They are deliberately manipulating their intuitive abilities to access information and therefore are developing stronger intuition, better mental telepathy and increased self-healing ability. Awareness increases the ease with which people can connect to the field. If a person is deliberately paying attention to their intuition, he or she will find it easier to make a connection to the field.

Each of us is unique insofar as the specific way in which we access the field of information, but the process is the same for everyone. For example, someone who thinks faster than someone else makes a more rapid connection, or someone who thinks more about a particular subject or object than others will have a stronger connection to that frequency of information. The combined energy of our interests, abilities and inclinations is our particular essence, you might say. What we focus on and what we are interested in gives us a greater understanding of what makes us who we are. It defines our uniqueness—our energy essence.

Our next step of awareness is global consciousness, where we all understand that what helps one of us helps us all. Only then can we understand that healing the planet is an extension of healing ourselves. We can actively participate in this evolution by understanding that our intentions affect things far beyond our conscious awareness. Individual consciousness, collective consciousness, global consciousness and universal consciousness are all the same. Here or there does not exist. Everything is here *and* there. Before or after does not exist. Everything *is*.

Would you elaborate on how our intention can manifest things in our lives such as finding a parking spot or getting a job?

By having the intention to get a job or even find a parking place, you are interacting with the field. You are part of the collective consciousness. This collective consciousness can influence events in ways that seem coincidental. Nevertheless, the collective consciousness is the interaction of every living organism's consciousness and aligns similar energy patterns.

Does the collective consciousness of all organisms in the universe have a tendency to influence events?

Yes, although the influence is subtle, rather than dramatic. Events are influenced in small and seemingly coincidental ways. When you look back on your life, think of all of the situations in which you noticed coincidences. You will begin to think that things happen for a reason. Part of what made events line up to produce coincidences is this collective consciousness.

Within this collective consciousness of all minds, how would you describe individual minds—my mind, your mind? Are we individuated somehow?

Yes and no. The intentions of everyone combined are functioning as one consciousness. This consciousness in turn influences everything else as we collectively form a web of connections. Imagine throwing a handful of pebbles into a pond. Even though every ripple from each pebble has a point of origin, the ripples will all connect and affect each other in countless ways. The ripples become one. So you could say we lose our individuality in how we affect other things. Every one of us and everything is affecting everything all the time. Yet there remain points of origin.

Is the collective consciousness past, present and future?

It is current, with the past definitely having some influence and the future being just a series of probabilities. When tapping into information about a future event, you are tapping into probabilities. All probabilities are in the field.

Chapter 6
Emotions and Attitude

Emotions can work for you or against you.
You can choose how they will affect you.

—ADAM

I've been asked many times what the root cause of disease is. Is it emotional, physical, spiritual or karma based? All of these aspects may interact to produce a health challenge. Emotions play an important role, one that we can influence.

Everyone reacts differently to events and experiences. Everyone experiences a range between happy and sad emotions. It is healthy to have a range of emotions. However, habitual negative feelings often contribute to physical illness. Many people whom I have worked on have a very strong emotional component to their physical ailment. In a great number of cases, the source of the problem is emotional: The health challenge is the physical manifestation of emotional baggage.

Just as emotions can intensify a health problem, they can also be used to alleviate many issues. Use your intentions to guide your emotions for the betterment of your health. I have noticed that some people who attend my workshops show signs of depression. The physical ailment may be at the root of the depression, or physical symptoms may be manifesting as a result of depression. Whichever the case may be, depression is intertwined with one's emotions, and emotions are inseparable from the physical body. It is important to realize that we can influence emotions and our reaction to them. Rather than spending time trying to decide which challenge appeared first, use energy to improve your state of mental and physical well-being.

I see depression as static patches of energy surrounding the head and shoulders. The patchy areas block the free flow of energy to the brain and nervous system. By resuming a harmonious patterned energy flow, the symptoms of the person's physical disorder or illness often lessen quickly. Just knowing that one has control positively affects one's emotional outlook. Mental and physical health cannot be separated in sickness or in health.

Attitudes about our health and healing are paramount to our wellness outcome. What we think and how we think about all experiences affect what we choose to do with our emotions. A woman I know attends every workshop I hold within 1000 miles of her home. When we first met, over two years ago, she had been given a terminal diagnosis by her doctor: Her cancer of the pancreas had spread to her lungs, liver and spleen. She was emotionally shattered. Since then, as a result of her diligently practicing the exercises given in my books and workshops, she has come to realize the influence she has on her own healing. Emotional and attitudinal self-reflection and change was a significant aspect on her journey to self-empowerment. A recent scan showed no evidence of any problem in her lungs, spleen or liver. Even the pancreatic tumor has shrunk. Knowing that her health has improved through her own doing makes her very proud. While the workshops help her to focus and stay on track, she feels self-empowered. Self-confidence radiates from her.

In this chapter, you'll find steps that will help you balance your emotions in a positive way. Doing this is an integral part of healing.

What are emotions and what purpose do they serve? How do they interact with the field of information? Emotions are feelings associated with intentions, thoughts and memories. The process emotions initiate is somewhat circular. Emotions function as the fuel for thoughts, or the fuel *of* thoughts. An intention, thought or memory stimulates neurons to emit light emissions—a specific frequency—which then connects to the field of information. This connection to the field instantaneously triggers the release of biochemicals; this in turn results in the manifestation of a specific emotion. The emotion expressed is specific to the particular frequency of light emitted (each of our emotions has a preset frequency that varies slightly from person to person), which in turn has a specific connection to the field. The manifestation of the emotion completes the circle.

Although emotions fuel and influence your intentions, they do not do so to a degree that overrides the intention. Intention remains the primary mechanism behind an action. Your intention activates neurons in the brain to send impulses from one neuron to another. This creates an electromagnetic field that resonates at a specific frequency. When you think a thought, a neuron resonates at a frequency that connects to the particular part of the field also resonating at that same frequency. In the body, the emotion related to that thought and the instantaneous connection to the field release biochemicals that fuel the expression of that emotion. From a subjective or experiential perspective, you feel the emotion as a sensation; by you feeling it, others around you can sense it or observe your expression of it also.

Emotions and their corresponding frequencies are complex. This complexity is due to the variations in a person's biological and chemical makeup. Our various types of measurements at present cannot measure emotions. We attempt to measure behavioral responses, breathing rates, biochemical levels and memory recall. Despite all these measurements, what remains most important is the attitude and interpretations we bring to this data. We have more control over these processes than we think.

Some people believe that emotionally charged intentions and their connection to the field figure prominently in the creation of our own reality. There is a lot of truth to this, particularly in the idea that we can influence our own physiology. You will tend to manifest those things on which your mind is set. Your attitude and focus not only will connect you to the field but will influence what actions you take in your everyday life.

Emotions can be a powerful healing tool when directed properly toward healing. They fuel our intentions, which activate physiological changes, of which the biochemical ones are the most well known. Each emotion triggers the release of different biochemicals. Certain biochemicals have opposing effects and so cancel out each other: When one molecule binds to another molecule with an opposing effect, any effect that either of those molecules alone would have caused will be nullified. This is the manner in which we can neutralize any unwanted effects from unproductive emotions. Through our focused intention of responding to emotions in a more balanced way, we can bring a healthier equilibrium to our biochemical systems. This is a vital part of what it means to be aware and to know yourself. This happens not by suppressing your emotions but by retraining your responses to them. You'll find steps to help you do this in the section Writing Your Own Ticket to Emotional Freedom, on page 110.

Because emotions have chemical correlates and specific energy patterns, they affect your physical health. The chemistry and energy of the body are entwined. Energy precedes the chemical reactions. Having a variety of emotions is healthy for the body in terms of energy, as balance is always the goal. It is human to have a wide range of emotions, rather than feeling an extreme of either anger, sadness or happiness all of the time. Indeed, we almost never experience one single emotion at a time. Even when an emotion is intense, other emotions are present. We can feel anger, sadness and happiness during the same event. All of us develop our own range of emotions that we are comfortable with. As we grow and change, our median point of emotional equilibrium will change.

Emotions are neither good nor bad in a moral or ethical sense, although some of them certainly make us feel bad. Emotions just are part of who we are. They come and go in a way that feels as though we have little control. But we do have control. Our thought patterns are the key to which emotions we feel. In addition, we can change or control how we react to our emotions. We can rationally decide how to evaluate and respond to our emotions in a balanced manner. It is important to become more aware of our emotions in order to recognize how we actually feel. Then we can decide how to react to the situation. Decide what your intentions are in that moment and that is how you can exercise control.

Health challenges often arise if a person gets stuck in negativity. Negative emotions will manifest into an unbalanced aura, or energy system. The healthy, flowing pattern of light emissions is being altered. This aura imbalance is a warning of physical problems. It indicates that detrimental chemical changes are occurring in the body because of toxic thoughts and emotions. With emotional challenges, such as depression, it is important to understand that you can influence control over your emotions and health.

Severe psychological and emotional disorders take particular forms in the aura. Schizophrenia usually appears as an aura with a sluggish-looking flow of light energy accompanied by spikes protruding and disappearing at random spots around the head. Once I began to work with this disorder in more depth, I noticed a particular energetic dysfunctional pattern. The initiation of a thought, which I see as a spark of light in the brain, gets derailed before it completes its path to form a completed thought, which I see as a pattern of light. This results in fragments of light shooting off in random directions. Thoughts get interrupted before they are completely processed.

As I mentioned previously, I see depression as patches of a static pattern of energy, similar to the snowy picture on a television screen when it is not tuned in to a station. These patches effectively block the free flow of energy.

Because emotions are feelings associated with intentions, thoughts and memories, they greatly assist us in recalling memories. When we experience an event, many neurons form a connection to the associated thoughts or pattern of thoughts, emitting light at certain specific frequencies. We have feelings or emotions about each event. Recalling an event simultaneously triggers the emotional association to it. Because of this, emotions can be used precisely in healing. Each emotion makes a strong connection to a particular region of the field. By being in control of your dominant emotions, you are controlling the information you are connecting to within the field. This in turn affects which frequencies of light remain prominent in your body and, consequently, which biochemicals are released to optimally affect your health.

Emotions of others also have an effect on us and on the wider collective energy of a group of people. This is why group healings are so powerful: The collective healing intentions and emotions of everyone in the group make the environment perfect for healing.

Suppose you are feeling neutral and not experiencing any strong emotions. Then someone in the room becomes angry with you. There is now a difference between your emotional state and that person's. Consequently, either you, or the other person or both of you will experience a shift in your feelings. You may not actually feel angry, but you will feel the difference between your frequency and that person's frequency. Many possibilities could occur at this point. You might become angry also, which results in the anger vibration level intensifying. Or you might intentionally move to a calming frequency level where you could influence the other's frequency to become more tranquil. Eventually a state of equilibrium will be reached. The two frequencies will tend to balance out or neutralize each other. Similarly, a non-angry person walking into a room of angry people can neutralize the intensity of the anger by emitting a calming emotion. This equilibrium will happen naturally with the introduction of a different vibration to the environment.

ACHIEVING EMOTIONAL EQUILIBRIUM

It is clear that emotions powerfully affect health. Take charge of your emotions. Only you have the power to do this. In this way, you can heal emotionally based problems. Everyone has emotional issues from their past, such as regrets involving relationships and forgiveness issues. It is how we handle them that impacts our daily lives. The past is over: We must leave it there as we move forward. We live in the present moment and are guided by our intentions, which are focused toward creating our future.

A woman I met was divorced many years before and had lost contact with her only son. As a result, she was emotionally unable to move forward. Although she remarried and had three more children within a stable, loving relationship, she was always thinking about her son. What was he doing? What was he thinking and saying? Would he ever question the negative stories about her that she was certain he was hearing? Would he ever try to find her?

Years ago she also developed fibromyalgia, a painful disorder causing stiffness and tenderness, so physical pain accompanied her psychological anguish. She attended one of my group workshops and found that as she gained control over her physical challenge through the use of positive intentions, she came to an understanding about her son. She practiced positive thinking as she imagined meeting her son as a young adult and getting to know and love him. She felt that he would feel this and respond in kind to her positive intentions.

A year later she attended another of my workshops. Through her tears she explained that she was no longer in any physical pain from fibromyalgia. And out of the blue her son had called her. They had met and now are catching up on the years that they missed together.

It is important to stay positive in order to project healing intentions accurately. This is not easy if you have recently received a negative medical diagnosis. Some people have told me that they found staying positive absolutely impossible. But nothing is impossible.

Start with imagining that you are in a positive frame of mind. Make a conscious effort to be optimistic and, before too long, it will become a habit: You will be naturally thinking this way. Don't forget to give yourself a pat on the back as you begin to notice changes in your perspective.

Writing Your Own Ticket to Emotional Freedom

This exercise will help minimize the impact on your daily life of all of the emotional difficulties you carry with you from your past.

1. Create a list of all the negative emotions your thought patterns tend to revisit. Make sure that you really have made an effort to dig deeply so that you leave no emotion buried.
2. Underline any themes you notice, as well as the repetitions of issues with no apparent solutions. You will be able to identify such issues by the negative self-talk phrases you habitually use, such as, "I always have trouble in relationships."

3. Now close your eyes and reflect on the issues and recurrent themes you have noted. In self-talk, what ideas do you reinforce? Question why you habitually have the thought. For instance, in reflecting on your use of the phrase "I always have trouble in relationships," you may not be sure whether this thought is a result of past events or whether your reality has been influenced by your negative thought.

4. Next, reflect on how your self-talk phrases and ideas can be expressed as positive changes. Identifying these issues is only the first step. Now you must actively work on modifying or eliminating them. The phrase "I always have trouble in relationships" leaves no room for positive change. Reword it in a positive framework, such as, "I am forming positive relationships with others."

5. Keep this list and, the following day, review each emotion and theme one at a time and reflect on it.

6. Think of what triggers this negative emotion in you. Then think of healthier ways to respond to the trigger event. When you hear yourself say aloud or in self-talk the same old line, "I always have trouble in relationships," catch yourself. Review what made you relate events to this statement that reinforces your negative thoughts and emotions.

7. In your mind's eye, re-create your reaction in this positive manner as realistically as possible. Set this new response as your emotional equilibrium goal. For instance, imagine the scenario of meeting a new person who shares many interests

with you and may become a friend. Leave yourself open to new possibilities, rather than maintaining the old habit of shutting the door before you see who is there.

8. Draw a line through each listed emotion that you have dealt with as you master your reaction to it. Enjoy the feeling of satisfaction and freedom from thoughts and emotions that don't serve your best interests.

Or, instead of trouble forming relationships, take road rage. In our time-challenged society, road rage sets many into irrational anger. If someone cutting you off in traffic sets you off into a rage, the next time this happens take a deep breath before reacting. Then imagine that the person in the other car is in a hurry to get to a friend at the hospital, or another such scenario that morally excuses the behavior. Chill your trigger by changing how you are going to react.

ADDICTIONS AND POOR LIFESTYLE HABITS

Our emotional reactions are a combination of two factors: our genetic makeup and environmental influences. Both are dynamic systems. We have all been raised in different environments, environments where our developing thoughts and emotions are guided by parental influences and everything else that we experience.

For some people, part of the explanation for health challenges lies in their first emotional experiences. In some family environments, it is expected that emotions be suppressed. If you were a boy, perhaps you were not permitted to cry. You may have been told to "suck it up" and "take it like a man." Some of us may have been told that we were stupid, or undeserving of what we wanted or needed, and thus we may be suppressing emotions of embarrassment, inadequacy or guilt. Addictions such as alcohol, drugs and smoking often can be tied to these denied emotions. And it is clear that physical symptoms and emotional reactions are often intertwined.

Addictions of various kinds are epidemic in the world. Addiction has physical, chemical and emotional factors. The pattern must be broken and the software reprogrammed to your benefit. In the long run, it doesn't matter what first caused the situation, as all the causes are intertwined. What is more important is analyzing the trigger, so that you can revise your reaction in order to negate those unwanted impulses. For instance, if stress sets off your smoking addiction, explore ways to decrease a specific stressor.

If a parent has a negative outlook, that energy influences everyone else in the household. Through the child's act of observing this behavior, he or she may develop poor emotional habits. The same may be said of any habit, such as smoking, drinking or overeating. Children can emulate the physical behaviors that they observe. You might be from a family in which all of the adults smoked. You can either accept this as being the norm, or reject it on the basis of what you have learned elsewhere. These are emotionally charged environmental factors that are obviously beyond your genetic makeup. Excessive stress and poor lifestyle habits can be deeply ingrained. One can have poor emotional habits as well as physical ones.

Your goal is to achieve and maintain emotional balance by retraining your responses to them.

Poor lifestyle habits can often be an underlying cause of health problems. Make it a priority to notice any issues that contribute to bad habits. The first step is to admit the existence of a problem. Understand what led you to a harmful habit or reaction so that you can retrain your responses at the emotional level. Reflect on emotional issues that go to the root of the problem. For example, if you overeat, ask yourself, why did I start overeating? Why do I let myself eat this way when I know it is unhealthy? Meditation may help you focus, with the intention of finding the answer.

Moving forward is not easy. First you must make peace with your past. Understand why you are currently facing this challenge. Learn from it so that you can effectively leave it where it belongs: in your past, not in your present or future. What feelings do you have to let go of in order to move forward? Do you need to forgive someone, or forgive yourself? Be honest in your self-reflection.

Your thoughts, emotions, words and behaviors determine the frequency of light you emit, and hence, all of your biochemical reactions. Your biophoton emissions react to your intentions; emotions fuel your intentions. Change is a complex process.

However, you are ultimately in charge. Just know that you *can* influence your emotions to achieve the level of wellness that you seek.

ADJUSTING YOUR ATTITUDE

If you doubt your ability to heal yourself, you must work on changing your attitude. It is important to realize that we are all healers. In this way, healing is demystified because each and every one of us embraces its power. We must become responsible for our own well-being. The mind, functioning as our computer, must know that we not only are serious about making changes but *are* making changes. Being honestly and consistently self-reflective is not easy in our chaotic modern society where there are so many distractions and so many potential stressors.

Many of us have grown accustomed to quick fixes as the solution to every difficulty that we encounter. For our health, we expect that there are pills to aid us. The same instant gratification is associated with having money. Even having a baby is sometimes viewed as the key to fixing a relationship. We are constantly searching elsewhere for the instant solution to our problems. With health and healing, look no further than yourself. You can make the difference.

A quick fix should not be your motivation for pursuing energy treatments. Imagine that you are given a prescription for an antibiotic that should be taken four times a day for ten days. After taking two pills, you feel no different so you stop taking them and declare that the antibiotic doesn't work. Yet, you haven't taken the whole course of antibiotics. It is important to follow directions in any treatment, whether conventional or alternative. It is pointless to judge the outcome if you haven't followed through on the process.

Or imagine that you become ill after drinking contaminated water, so you take all of the antibiotics your doctor prescribed. Immediately after finishing the course, you drink water from the same contaminated source. As a result, you become ill once again. Is the treatment to blame if you haven't changed the habits that contributed to your illness in the first place? Keep this in mind as you follow your chosen healing path so you don't repeat what created your health challenge.

When illness strikes, it is natural to feel worried and fearful. This results in a lot of anxiety. Family members and close friends also feel the stress. This can lead to further complications that prolong the negative impact that the health challenge has on you. Well-meaning family members and friends may find it difficult to be positive even when you want to make changes for the better. It is very important that those around you be supportive and positive with you. Their intentions will affect yours. Be genuine when deciding to empower yourself. You know the difference between being truly positive in your outlook and sugarcoating a negative attitude.

Remember that you can change yourself. You can change your thinking patterns. Fear blocks the flow of helpful information needed to initiate your transformation to wellness. Go forward, leaving any doubts and fears behind.

Your level of education is not a factor in your ability to become self-empowered and develop your potential to change. I have spoken to many people well educated in mainstream Western medicine who have a hard time changing their attitudes and who doubt a person's ability to really change. It is important that you are able to feel and know that change is forthcoming. Our challenge is to forget what we have learned, and remember what we have forgotten.

Steps to Achieving a Positive Attitude

1. Notice your attitude toward change. Decide to expect change, then welcome it and enjoy it. As with any experience in life, there is a direct relationship between what we put into it and what we get out of it. Be willing to modify your unproductive attitudes.

2. Forgiveness is an essential part of cleansing negative emotions and removing unproductive attitudes. This includes forgiving others as well as ourselves. Past mistakes should be left in the past. As the forgiver, empower yourself to let go.

3. Live freely in the present. Learn from past experiences, and dismiss as nonhappenings any worries of possible future events. Concentrate your energies on the here and now and make the most of it. What you do now creates your future.

Focus on thinking, feeling and being in the present moment. Step up to the challenge.

We all have different filters through which we perceive our experiences. Sometimes these filters so totally block the incoming information that they become blinders. I call this "an intellectual block," as the person—either consciously or subconsciously—is not receptive to new incoming information at that time. For such a person, self-reflective work is required before he or she can be receptive to change. Rather than thinking about the change, it is more effective to *feel* the change. The next step forward is knowing that you are on the road to recovery. The *mind* is programmable by word and thought, and the body will follow.

We all have receptors that can receive these subtle energies, but they must be ready to receive, connect and vibrate as they absorb new information. Even harmless, innocuous distractions can interfere with tuning in to subtle energies. Some people are preoccupied with watching their favorite TV shows, to the exclusion of all other shows. We can only effectively watch one program at a time, so by watching it we effectively block all other incoming information. We must be ready and willing to shed old habits in order to allow ourselves to receive and process new incoming information.

I recently attempted a distant healing requested by a woman with impressive academic credentials. She was extremely well

Illustration 1:
The black bird I encountered in the forest, just like the one
I had seen in my vision.

Illustration 2: Ripples of energy in empty space before the Big Bang.

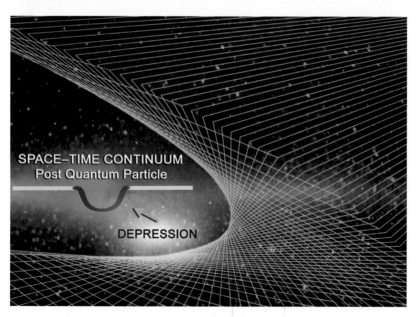

Illustration 3: The manifestation of the first particle of matter created a depression in the space–time continuum; the particle's tiny gravitational force was enough to initiate the Big Bang.

Illustration 4:
Local telepathy involves a direct exchange of light emitted from one person and influencing another person.

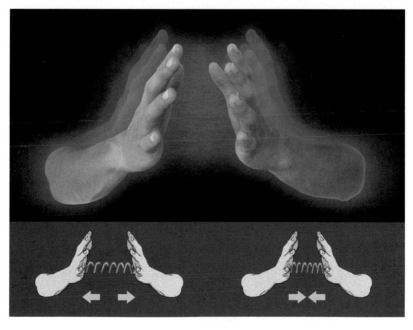

Illustration 5:
Feel your energy.

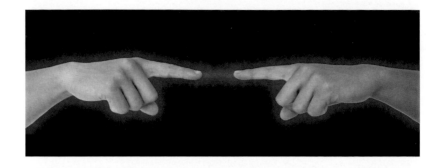

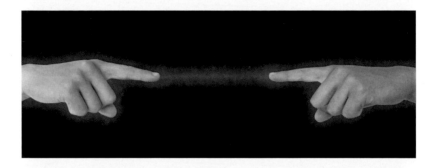

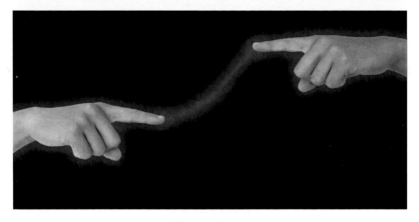

Illustration 6:
See your energy.

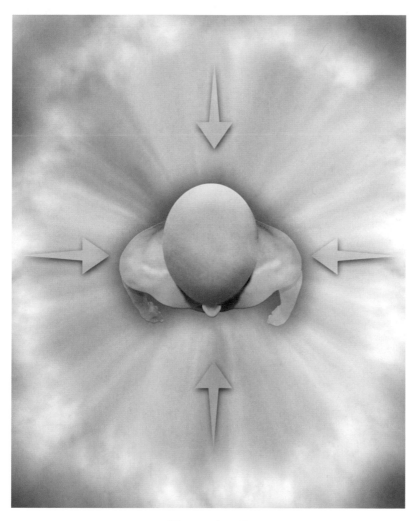

Illustration 7:
Bird's-eye view of bringing in universal energy.

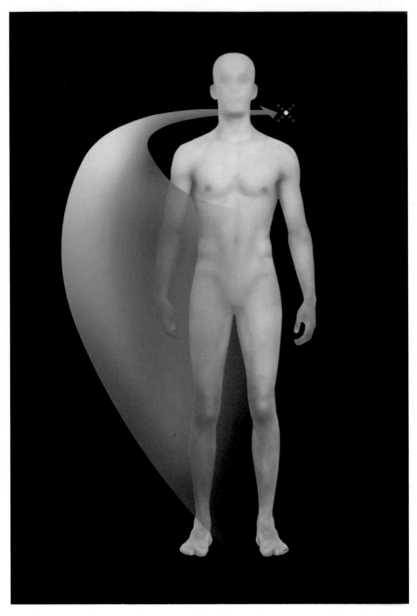

Illustration 8:
Seeing an aura: Focus on a spot behind the person.

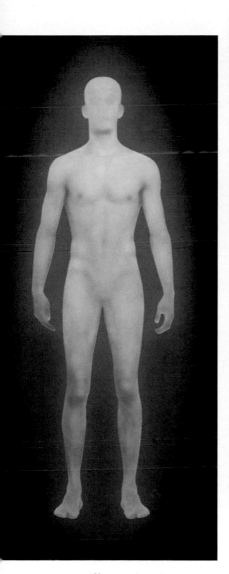

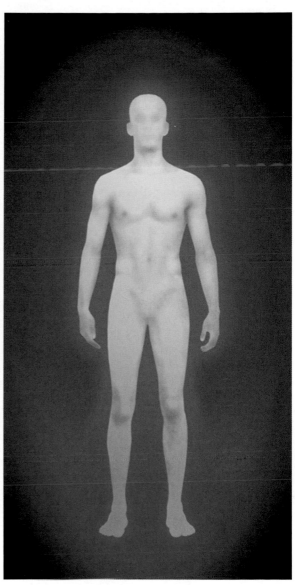

Illustration 9:
A slight, shimmering aura.

Illustration 10:
An aura with defined, flowing colors.

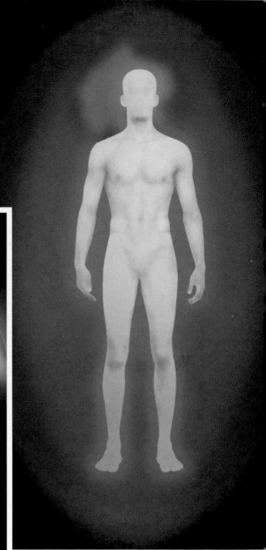

Illustration 11:
A break in the aura,
in the head area.

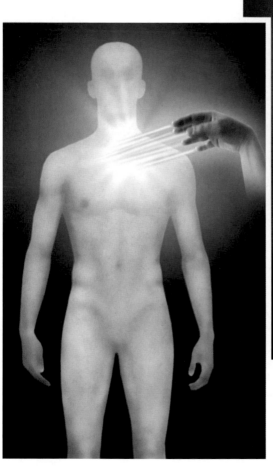

Illustration 12:
Comb your energy by visualizing light
extending from your fingertips; use it to
give yourself a massage of light energy.

Illustration 13:
Light being absorbed during the formation of a chemical bond.

Illustration 14:
Light being emitted during the breaking of a chemical bond.

Illustration 15:
A quantum object disappears at one location and by interacting with the field, it reappears at another location without having traveled through the intervening space.

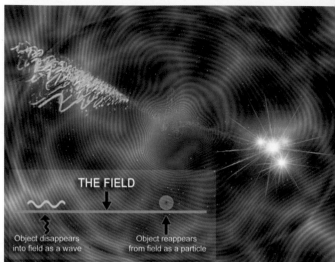

THE FIELD

Object disappears
into field as a wave

Object reappears
from field as a particle

Illustration 16:
DNA interacting with and emitting light. Energy as light information is dynamic; with every intention, you are emitting light that influences your DNA.

Illustration 17:
Thought as light being transferred along neural pathways. Thought interacts nonlocally as it radiates to and absorbs information from the field.

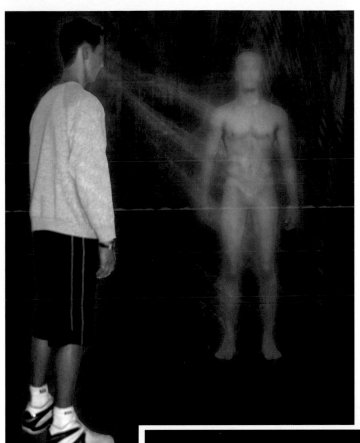

Illustration 18:
Projecting a
holographic
image.

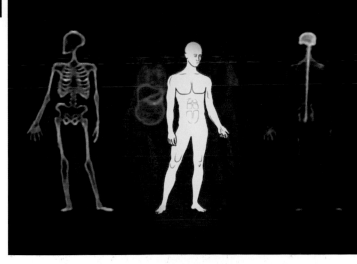

Illustration 19:
Various holographic views. Access these subsets of
information for healing.

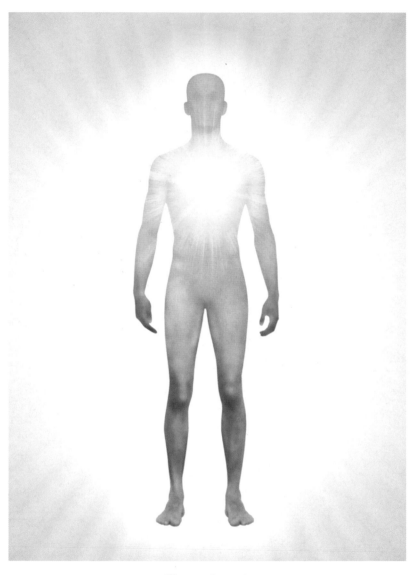

Illustration 20:
Light-hearted visualization:
Collect light in your heart area; then radiate it to every cell
as you become as bright as the sun.

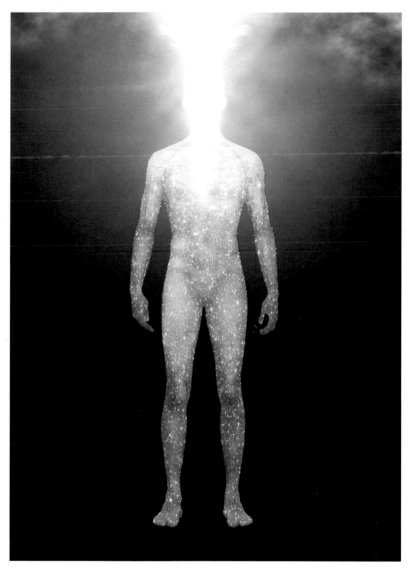

Illustration 21:
Lightbulb visualization:
Cells beginning to resonate at a coherent frequency;
soon your entire body will vibrate with a harmonious light.

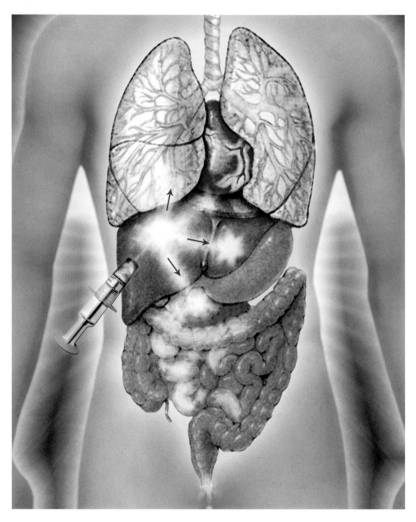

Illustration 22:
Light injections visualization:
Inject light directly into the problem area, allowing the healing
light to radiate to surrounding tissue.

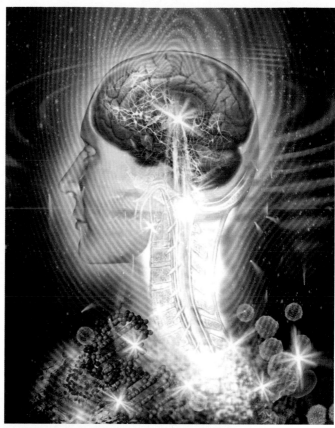

Illustration 23:
Bright white light visualization: Light the center of your brain with your internal light source and let it grow light energy roots that connect to every cell in your body.

Illustration 24:
Bubble wrap visualization: Breathe healing light energy into each cell-pocket; with exhalation, burst as many bubbles as you can, popping away your problem.

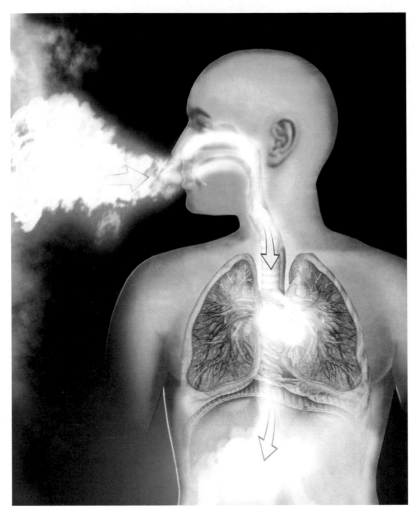

Illustration 25:
Mythical dragon breathing visualization:
With inhalation, imagine that you are breathing in white, hot
flames; focus on moving these flames to your place of stress.

read in alternative healing. I was puzzled when she felt minimal effects after the treatments. When she told me a third time how she thought she had got her ailment, a light dawned. Apparently she saw herself as a victim. She was blaming someone else for being responsible for all of her health problems. But her victim mentality was not serving her well. Blame undercuts self-empowerment. A me-versus-them perspective not only is a futile attempt to separate oneself from others but it shifts responsibility away from oneself. This woman's attitude left her with nonproductive negative thoughts that interfered with her self-healing.

Once you have done your emotional clearing and have let go of outdated beliefs, step away from your rational, analytical role and move to an awareness of feeling your energy. Analysis, with all of its argumentative chatter, causes resistance to the natural course of information as energy. Just let the energy flow.

PACKING FOR YOUR HEALING JOURNEY

Dealing with emotional and psychological baggage can be a daunting task. A relatively easy way to tackle it is to imagine you are packing for your healing journey. You have one backpack to carry with you, so it would be wise to bring only the essentials you need along the way. Examine carefully what you are taking. Be selective. Take only what you need. What you are leaving behind is every emotion, thought, feeling or memory that you do not need. Think of these as bricks that only weigh you down.

Bricks can also create a wall, which may be comforting in its familiarity but will hinder your journey forward. What you don't need must be left behind—or rejected and deflected away from yourself.

If you find that your backpack is too heavy to carry, open your mental backpack and take a close look to see if it is weighed down by negative emotions such as:

- Doubt about your own ability to influence your health.
- Uncertainty about the power of subtle energy.
- Hesitation about your commitment or that of those around you on your path to wellness.

Every one of these thoughts is a stone in your backpack, weighing you down. Assess each belief or thought that is holding you back from achieving your goal:

1. Pick up one stone (i.e., negative emotion or attitude) at a time.
2. Identify the belief or event that is causing you to express this emotion or attitude.
3. Say out loud what it is and why you don't need it anymore.
4. In your mind's eye, throw the "stone" as far away from you as you can.
5. Turn away from where it lands. Turning away leaves every stone isolated and powerless.

6. Repeat this process until you are no longer carrying any unnecessary baggage. You will soon realize that all you need to pack for your journey is universal energy and your own imagination. In fact, what you need is both limitless and weightless, so you don't really need a backpack at all.

If emotional issues are not dealt with, then an energy treatment will be like stretching an elastic band. It seems as though the person is accepting the energy, but he or she is unable to process the incoming information. The person is not receptive to receiving. The elastic stretches, but it retracts to its original shape and there is no lasting benefit from the treatment. This is why it is essential to focus on emotional issues that may be blocking your way forward.

How effectively you can do this emotional clearing depends on how flexible in your thinking you are. A woman contacted me for advice on energy healing, and I suggested this exercise to her. She considered herself already well informed in energy work and when I asked her what she would pack, she told me that she planned to take along some of her favorite books for her healing journey. It seemed to me that she was using these books to find emotional comfort in familiarities from her past, an attitude that did not lend itself to an open-minded approach to her future. She became incensed when I suggested that she might need to be more receptive to change in order for her healing path to lead to lasting benefits. While her academic knowledge base could have been valuable background information, her rigid dependence on it had become a block against moving forward.

TAKING TIME OUT

Without even being aware of it, we all can become preoccupied with the daily routine of our lives. Sometimes it is beneficial to step back and take stock. Evaluate where you are in relation to your goals. Take time out to relax—or play basketball. Give yourself permission to just hang out. You don't need to justify every waking moment on some sort of linear productivity scale. Take a break from your schedule.

Relaxation is vital to our well-being, so it is important to find leisurely pastimes or exercise routines. Many people find meditation a wonderfully stress-reducing exercise. It relaxes our minds and bodies by resetting our conscious awareness. Whatever you find to be an enjoyable way to unwind, set aside time for it. Many of us feel that we don't have enough time as it is, so how could we possibly set time aside for "doing nothing"? Change your thinking on this, because downtime should be a priority in our busy lives. Grab your calendar and schedule more relaxation time. Restructure something in your life so you are free for this essential activity.

HOW HUMOR AND GRATITUDE AFFECTS HEALTH AND HEALING

Humor is necessary because it reminds us to view life on its lighter side. There are many documented cases of people improving their health just by adding humor to their lives. A few laughs a day are wonderful medicine for the soul. Even something as simple as watching a silly TV show after dealing with the more serious issues in life will be beneficial.

And finally, be grateful for life. Learn to be content with what you do have, rather than dwelling on what you do not have. This applies to material objects, relationships and health. Appreciation brings happiness. Life should be enjoyed. Being continually grateful is perhaps life's greatest challenge. The simple act of saying thanks before a meal is a good way to express gratitude for what we have. Another simple act is to every day acknowledge one thing for which you are thankful. Each morning say aloud what aspect you appreciate about that particular day. Another part of gratitude is returning positive energy to others. Did you go out of your way to make someone else's day a better one? Practice gratitude until it is habitual. Before you realize it, you will have established a new attitude. Then you will be able to attract into your life everything and everyone that you need. The shift to this balanced attitude toward life is in your hands.

Reset your goal of overall health to its maximum potential. Absorb into every fiber of your being what you need to achieve this. You will feel changes taking place as this shift toward healing starts to happen in your mind and body. Deflect outward by throwing away what you don't need on the path toward this goal. Now you are ready for your journey.

When you put emotion into a thought or intention, does that always give that thought or intention more influence on your reality?

It depends what the thought and the emotion are. If they are aligned with each other, then the intention is being amplified, sometimes very powerfully. In that case, the influence would be greater. However, if you have an intention with a conflicting emotion and they are not working together, the intention is less effective. For instance, your intention is to remain calm in traffic. But you get cut off and you react in anger. As you become more aware of your trigger to anger, your intention to react calmly will become more effective.

Does fear block the flow of information?

Nothing can actually block information. Fear can divert your attention. Fear might deflect or redirect other information from coming to the forefront, making more important information seem less important. For example, if you are afraid of snakes, that fear will be your singular focus if one is near you. This might prevent you from noticing that you are dangerously close to a moving car while trying to get away from the snake. As a result of fear, you might not pick up on what is more essential for you at that time.

How do we know if our healing intentions are sincere when we are assessing our emotions and attitudes?

Sometimes it is difficult to know if we are sincere in our intentions. Subconscious conflicts that might undermine a seemingly sincere intention to get well could be common issues such as economic or social concerns. No one knows you better than you do. Pay attention to how you think; notice your habits, attitudes and the emotional patterns in which you think. Try to understand your subconscious mind the best you can. In a relaxed meditative state, ask yourself, are these intentions sincere? Reflect honestly on your answer.

Do animals have emotions?

Pet owners swear that their pets have emotions. At least, pet owners read into their pets' behavior a wide range of emotions. Domestic pets constantly interact with the actions and emotions of their owners. This is why we become so emotionally attached to our pets: We carry on a constant emotional dialogue with them. Humans are not unique when it comes to having emotions. We simply express them differently than most other animals.

Chapter 7
Beliefs and Spirituality

Intention and expectation of outcome guide our reality.

—ADAM

Three years ago, I started working with a woman who had pancreatic cancer. She traveled from the Canadian province of Ontario to Saskatchewan to see me at the First Nations International Healing and Medicines Gathering in which I was participating. At this gathering I had my own teepee in which to conduct my healing groups. It held twelve people at a time. I began working with the woman in the group setting of my teepee. Doctors had told her the cancer was terminal and estimated that in a few months she would be in palliative care. We worked intensively in that week of the Gathering, but I told her that she would need to assume responsibility for her own healing. I could guide her occasionally, but I would be unavailable to do individual treatments with her when I returned to school that fall.

Since then, she has made many changes in her life. I emphasized to her what I teach everyone. It is imperative to examine every aspect of your life and undertake major destressing. Allow only positive self-talk to filter in. She now does qigong, yoga, meditation and positive visualizations and affirmations. She has made it her full-time preoccupation to get well, and this attitude has paid off.

Before we met, her oncologists said her pancreatic tumors were growing rapidly and that her next scan likely would show that they had spread to the liver. Instead, the next scan showed a 25 percent reduction in tumor size, with no metastasizing. More than two years later, the tumors have almost disappeared. She feels wonderful and maintains her own self-healing program.

Everyone has the ability to self-heal; we just have to learn how to use it. Healing of body, mind and spirit is true healing. Energy healing requires flexibility for change and participation.

Every one of us views our world subjectively, that is, from within our individual belief systems. We form our opinions through life experiences, religious beliefs, and spiritual and cultural views. Our beliefs and disbeliefs act as filters through which we view everything. They set the limitations that guide our thoughts, words and actions. This is true of scientists, too, of course. Their reality is based on their subjective biases. This is an important point to understand, since scientists play a major role in shaping society's accepted theories of reality. Most often what scientists conclude in experiments is based on the pre-existing and accepted theories that are part of the subjective viewpoint of the scientists in the first place. In other words, they prove what they already "know" to be true.

As children, we see life only in the present moment. Consequences for our actions can be envisioned only as some obscure possibility in a vague and distant reality. Children feel a certain way and react intuitively in the here and now. They have not yet developed an analytical process which interferes with intuition. By the time they are adults, they will have had years of societal training which limits imagination and dictates acceptable beliefs and behaviors. This is achieved through parental role modeling, the school system and other cultural, social and religious practices. These influences mold our reality. Prior to this conditioning, everything and anything is possible.

We have all been young children—that is, spontaneous beings—at one point in our lives. It is important to regain that boundless imagination that we all still have within us. The ultimate in flexible thinking is allowing ourselves to know this. The most important aspect of remembering our spontaneous selves is, as with our emotions, to forget what we have learned and remember what we have forgotten.

Each of us faces challenges in life. Most of us are not very old before we have some sort of health concern to deal with. There are many other things in life, such as relationships, school and work, that require our attention as well. Beliefs are fundamental in each of these. We all know someone who approaches any challenge with a positive outlook. Time seems to reward these people with an etched-on, permanent smile, rather than a worried frown. It is not that they have traveled through life unscathed. It is that they see every event in its most positive light. Our outlook and expectations stem from our beliefs.

In health issues, expecting to get better is a huge step toward recovery. Imagine two patients who are facing the same dire health challenge, one in which a statistical survival rate of 50 percent looms over them. One of the patients is almost always optimistic, seeing the proverbial glass as half full, and expects to be one of the patients who fully recovers. The other is usually pessimistic, seeing the glass as half empty, and doubts whether she will be one of the patients who survives. Which person would you expect to survive if all other factors are the same? Most of us would expect the optimist to survive, because he expects to.

This optimistic belief is often described in an almost mystical sense as the will to live. What exactly is the will to live? It is a self-declaration of the intent to survive. It is the unwavering belief that this will happen. When you expect a positive outcome, you send that intention within yourself and beyond yourself via biophoton emissions, initiating a cascade of biochemical reactions in the body that will maximize the possibility of this event actually occurring. Your thought has set everything in motion to achieve what you expect to happen. And guess what? Your positive thinking does influence events.

We all innately possess this limitless power within ourselves. Our bodies do listen to what we tell them. All we have to do is ensure that we are sending out the optimum signal for our wellness. The constant reinforcement of our beliefs does impact us by either setting a healing pattern in place or by emphasizing and strengthening an established negative response.

Think of your mind as a computer that can be programmed to enhance your growth and well-being to their optimum. Maximize the functioning of your immune system by programming yourself to ensure your healthy future.

Before this can happen, you have to want to change. It sounds easy. Of course you want to get better. But it has to be more than idle talk. Your mind and body will recognize whether or not you are ready and willing to make changes. If you are not, the intentions are not sincere and will be viewed and dismissed by your body as background noise.

If you are attempting to feed yourself the same old unproductive self-talk and thought patterns—and just sugarcoat them—think again. For instance, if you are telling yourself that right after summer vacation you will start an exercise program, what you are really saying is that these changes are not important enough for you to start now. You are attempting to fool yourself, and that will never work. You are too smart for that. Who knows you better than yourself? You can't fool yourself, but you *can* change yourself.

Your sincere intention must be your singular focus. This can be accomplished by becoming self-reflective and totally honest with yourself. Your conscious desire must be synchronized with your subconscious thoughts and beliefs. Ask yourself, "What do

I want?" Limit yourself to one desired outcome. If your answer is that you want to be healthy again, say so. If you want to live, say it aloud. Shout, "I want to live!" Let it resonate within you that this is your intention. This is what you expect. Change any habits or patterns that are not in synchronicity with this new program. Let yourself know that you are seriously focused on the path toward change.

When doing your self-healing work, you must maintain your focus on your positive intentions of change. While doing so, you may wonder if what you are doing is working. If you are practicing the following four steps, your self-reflective work should bring you answers right away:

1. You make time to reflect on your goals and intentions in a relaxed state of mind.
2. You make time for the emotional equilibrium exercises outlined in Chapter 6.
3. You reflect on your healing beliefs during relaxation.
4. You do the affirmations outlined below.

Must a person believe in energy healing in order for it to work? It certainly speeds along changes if you do believe that you can be well again. You do need to be positive and have an open mind. A positive attitude is very important for any type of healing process to be successful, whether you pursue conventional or alternative treatments, or both. It is a skill to achieve this level of control of one's attitude. But remember: A closed mind is locked from within. Like everything else in life, the shape of your future is ultimately your decision and your choice. Now you have belief and intention directed toward healing. You can now expect change to happen. Everything is set into motion, and you know that your positive outcome will occur.

Change is a choice. This responsibility is our own. Most adults understand that they are accountable for their own actions, including habits. What is more of a challenge is recognizing that we are responsible for every thought, word and belief as well. Go beyond any blame, whether it is focused inward at yourself or outward at someone else. Blame and guilt are totally unproductive.

Imagine the process of change already taking place within you. Practicing the appropriate visualizations for you (see Part 3) will help you actualize this shift. Your imagination is limitless, so use it to program change. Make the time to do visualizations: They are an essential part of reprogramming. No matter how busy you are, make reprogramming a priority. Programming for positive change is your decision and your doing. Take responsibility and you will receive all of the resulting benefits.

AFFIRMATIONS

Affirmations are short statements of belief which can be said aloud or in your thoughts for the purpose of empowering yourself. They help change existing beliefs that may be holding you back from reaching your potential—in any aspect of your life. Affirmations also reinforce positive beliefs that you may need to strengthen. On your path to wellness, they help you realize your maximum healing ability.

A major health challenge can be overwhelming. It may be the first time in your life that you can't be healed by a quick visit to the doctor and a prescription. A crisis calls for change. Whatever the ailment, it has been brewing for some time before it is evident through symptoms or diagnosis. Once the symptoms manifest or the illness is diagnosed, it can no longer be ignored.

This call for action can be a positive life-altering experience. How you react to your health challenge is your choice. Be proactive rather than reactive, and embrace necessary changes. Look at it as an opportunity to take charge of your life and health. Create affirmations of self-acceptance and self-empowerment; I've given you some examples below. As with visualizations, your affirmations are particular to your needs and challenges. The more you customize these examples, the more effective they will be.

Set aside a specific time in your day for doing affirmations. If you do them first thing in the morning, they will set a positive tone for your entire day. Look into a mirror and make eye contact with yourself. You expect others to look you in the eye when they are addressing you, so extend the same courtesy to yourself. Focus on the words as you express them aloud with feeling:

I love myself.
I love others and others love me.
I am happy with who I am and what I think, say and do.
I feel wonderful and am full of healing energy.
Today is a marvelous day full of new opportunities.

Those of you saying, "Yeah, sure, but I don't really like myself," do this anyway. Intend to begin liking yourself. Practice self-forgiveness and monitor your behavior as you begin to change.

The power of the mind over functions of the body is widely acknowledged. The power of the mind over the body has been observed in medical studies to measure treatment efficacy: Patients often improve even when the pill they are taking is only a sugar pill. This is because they believe the pill they are taking will heal them. This phenomenon is known as the placebo effect. In fact, in drug trials, the health improvements in the placebo group are often as significant as those in the group receiving the actual drug.

You undoubtedly have heard of people who have a dissociation disorder that results in multiple personalities. One personality may exhibit totally different characteristics from another. Therapists who work with these patients report that one personality is able to have a medical condition independently of the others. For example, an allergy, eczema or even asthma exhibited in one personality may not exist in another personality. Each personality believes it is a separate person to the extent that each has separate physical characteristics, including medical conditions. The existence of varying medical conditions in the same physical body illustrates the incredible power of beliefs and expectations of our minds, as all personalities are within the same physical body. We all have this level of control of our mind-body; we just have to harness its benefits.

Because beliefs are so powerful, healing must be participatory. Give yourself positive affirmations. Meditate and reflect. Regain harmonious balance in your life. Having supportive people around you is important, but the bottom line is that you yourself must be ready and willing to make the necessary changes to improve your own health.

THE INFLUENCE OF BELIEFS ON MY HEALING WORK

Years ago, a loving mother contacted me seeking help for her teenage son. He was diagnosed with obsessive-compulsive disorder (OCD). People with this affliction often overemphasize perfection and a need for orderliness. They engage in repetitious compulsive behavior, such as constant hand washing because of fear of germs, or constant checking of electrical appliances to make sure they have been unplugged. Repeated blinking and facial tics are OCD symptoms of anxiety. In severe cases, the person is unable to function in society because the behavior rituals consume the entire day. Leaving the house for an errand can be as challenging as planning a climb to the top of Mount Everest.

Recognizing the complexity of the disorder was a good start in helping their son, and the teenager's parents were certain that he would be receptive to my suggestions. I had never seen what OCD looked like on the energetic level, so I was eager to take a look at his photograph to see what I could do.

I could see that OCD appears on the aura as loops of information that are never fully processed. This loopiness is an intuitive feel I got from the aura more than it is an actual appearance. I realized that the boy would benefit from doing a calming visualization and meditation, which would allow the repetitive information loops to synchronize into smoother energy flow throughout the aura. The goal would be to tune the untuned behavioral habits by regaining a more orderly flow of thoughts.

When I replied that I would work with the young man, his response was unexpected. The parents were more surprised than I was. Their son was not interested in distant treatments. His disconcerting response was that he was afraid of losing the OCD. Despite the challenges it presented, it was a known quantity. He defined himself through the disorder and had learned to wear it somewhat comfortably. Obviously, he was not open to change at that point.

This young man's belief that his affliction was an integral part of him raises an interesting point. Every one of us must take an objective look at ourselves and ask, how does this illness serve my needs? It sounds like a ridiculous question until you answer it honestly. Does this ailment give you permission to relax more, or to get out of obligations that you would otherwise have to face reluctantly? Does it serve any purpose in your relationships with others?

People with addictions often view their habit as being an integral part of themselves. Such beliefs are intensified and compounded not only by how we perceive ourselves but by how we believe others view us. This can make change even more of a challenge. Yet, each of us has the ability to accomplish anything that we set our minds to. Do not fall into the trap of labeling yourself or living by a label imposed by others. Move beyond it. Only you can decide your future, through the choices you make.

Another belief that blocks healing is that of being a victim. A man who came to me with Lyme disease repeatedly told me the sequence of events leading to his contracting the disease. He blamed a friend who owned the cottage where he had been bitten by the infected tick. Yet, before being bitten, he was constantly thinking about being bitten and was desperately afraid of contracting Lyme disease. It didn't occur to him that he was attracting the course of events through his focused thought signals about being bitten by a tick and getting ill. He repeatedly imagined himself being bitten, and his belief in the outcome contributed to it becoming reality.

In his mind, however, he was a victim. He was not interested in changing any of the beliefs he had, as doing so would threaten his position as an innocent bystander who was wronged. He believed that he needed rescuing, and he wanted someone else to heal him. This belief kept him stuck in the past because he couldn't get beyond the "if onlys": If only he had not been invited to the friend's cottage; if only he had been informed about the prevalence of ticks in the area.

When I spoke to him about how he could change his perspective on what occurred, he became defensive to the point of hostility. He considers himself a victim. This man will experience the help he needs when he becomes open to a significant change in his beliefs. When he is able to accept responsibility for his own choices, and forgive his friend and himself, he will be able to move forward. Only then will he be able to make any significant progress in his own healing.

Many people have been injured in car accidents when someone else was driving. The driver didn't have the intention to harm anyone. If this is your situation, you must try to leave the establishing of fault to the lawyers and courts. Concentrate on getting well. Make sure that being a victim is only a legal term, and not an emotional state for you.

Life consists of a series of choices. The book of "if onlys" is the longest book on the shelf. Leave it there gathering dust. Those possibilities did not occur. One cannot dwell on the past and fully focus on the present at the same time. Let it be, and move on into the present. This is a choice that you make with every thought, word and deed.

It is important that you understand the participatory nature of healing; that is, your role in your healing. I have held many workshops across North America in order to teach self-empowering techniques for healing. My emphasis in these workshops is how you can better manage your own health concerns, rather than how I can solve them for you. Each workshop session has at least one group energy treatment. This enables all participants to feel the connection to our universally common energy source. Feeling this energy shift is often what is needed for someone to believe that a change is possible. I suggest tools, such as the visualizations in Part 3, that enable participants to continue their healing process independently. The workshops are intended to strengthen the self-confidence needed to assist in self-healing.

I cannot emphasize enough how important it is to become aware of your recurring thoughts and your beliefs and to be open to new information and change. You will attract and experience whatever it is that you consistently expect to manifest. As I mentioned, in my workshops I often do several aura readings, on volunteers among the participants. The accuracy of the aura readings is usually immediately confirmed by the participant. It is interesting to note some of the exceptions. Once again, one's focus, based on one's beliefs, enter into the picture. The aura of one particular man showed a problem with his sciatic nerve. When I pointed that out, he did not concur. He had prostate cancer for which he had undergone surgery. Later, however, he told me that he has experienced severe sciatic pain on and off for over thirty years. He had forgotten about that ailment because his singular focus was on the prostate cancer: He was so preoccupied with the possibility that the cancer would show in his aura that he could think of nothing else.

Another man's aura showed a problem in his abdominal area. He told me that he had diabetes and that I hadn't correctly identified his health challenge. However, he is taking insulin, so his blood sugar levels appeared normal. The aura is simply an external reflection of what is happening inside the body. An aura reading gives general, cursory information. I can more specifically see a problem with the pancreas when I "go in" for a treatment, a more involved process than reading the aura. Even though the pancreas is in the abdominal area, where I said a problem was indicated, the man expected more detail than the aura provides. He had one answer in mind—diabetes—and heard nothing related to or beyond that.

Outside of the workshops, I have worked with people in comas who are unable to communicate their wishes and beliefs. At this point, the wishes of the closest relatives must be respected, and so their beliefs and expectations play an important role in the healing process. A supportive family who accepts energy healing will, through their positive intentions, amplify the healing intentions that I send during a treatment. In this way, others play a direct role in the process of healing.

Sometimes our limiting beliefs stem from the statements of health professionals. It is traumatic enough to be diagnosed with cancer. To be told it is terminal is devastating. This news can become a self-fulfilling prophecy. We might see our situation as hopeless and mentally set ourselves on a course toward death. While we are all going to die eventually, the question is when— and how we choose to live until that time. We all can improve our quality of life through attention to mind, body and spirit.

I treated a woman who had been diagnosed years earlier with multiple myeloma. She has consistently worked on influencing her health through visualizations and energy treatments, and now tests negative for cancer. When her test results first showed that there was no evidence of cancer, this wonderful news was quickly dismissed by the doctors. She was told, "The cancer is gone for now, but it will be back." It is difficult for a person to stay with their program of positive self-healing intentions when faced with dire predictions. Remember that nobody knows for certain what the future holds for any of us. There is no doubt that you have more to do with your own future than anyone else does. Her doctors now refer to this woman as their miracle patient.

Another woman with pancreatic cancer has been working on influencing her own health through visualizations and energy treatments at workshops. Over two years ago, she was given a terminal diagnosis: The cancer was growing rapidly and was by now evident in her liver and lungs as well. A recent scan revealed that her liver and lungs were clear and the pancreatic tumor had shrunk, but her doctor told her that the radiologist did not include this fact in his report. Within his framework of beliefs, the tumor could not have shrunk, and therefore it had. If the woman's positive health result had come about through Western medical intervention rather than a patient's own energy work, the radiologist probably would have been more inclined to believe what he saw. The results were actually so positive that her doctors have spoken to her about rewriting her medical history as a possible misdiagnosis in the first place. I congratulate all of those people who have achieved this level of improvement.

Many times I have observed how beliefs can influence diagnoses. For some health practitioners, it is easier to change the diagnosis than it is to change their beliefs. The goal posts can be moved. Most people see the medical diagnosis they receive as an indisputable and unwavering fact. Yet, the diagnosis often seems to be flexible when a condition improves by means other than Western medicine. In cases where energy healing produces positive results, I have heard responses from skeptical health professionals such as:

- We were wrong about it being terminal cancer in the first place, because the patient has survived.
- It wasn't cancer at all. It just looked like a malignant tumor. But it couldn't have been because its behavior is not consistent with that diagnosis since the tumor has shrunk or disappeared.

- The spinal cord wasn't completely severed as was previously thought. It must have been only partially severed, because some feeling and mobility has been regained.
- Pain is a subjective experience and therefore we cannot possibly determine whether it has actually decreased or not.
- The brain damage could not have been as severe as we thought or a full recovery could not have occurred.

I am no longer concerned about these medical interpretations. What matters is that a person's physical, emotional and spiritual health improves.

If you have been diagnosed with a serious illness, make sure the diagnosis is not blinding everyone, including yourself, to other unrelated illnesses you might also have. For example, I knew a woman who had pancreatic cancer but died of an untreated bowel obstruction. Everyone treating her was cancer-blind: They couldn't get past this six-letter word on her chart in order to consider other conditions she might also have.

Patients themselves can do better at informing their health providers of all healing disciplines they are involved in. Many people don't bother discussing alternative therapies they are using with their medical doctors and, conversely, the naturopathic practitioner doesn't always hear about the allopathic (Western) medical choices a person faces. This fractured health care system, which has not optimally served the needs of the health consumer, is slowly changing.

Despite the fact that many health professionals continue to view the body as made up of separate mechanical parts, I have been encouraged by the opening of minds I have seen within the medical community. Patients want a doctor with two ears—one to hear the holistic needs, and the other to hear the allopathic needs—so that their health needs can be addressed without conflict. As enlightened consumers become more informed and demand change, health professionals are seeking to better understand our mind-body connections and thus are beginning to reflect a holistic awareness.

Alternative and complementary medicine is beginning to integrate with allopathic medicine. This is known as "integral medicine." The mainstream media is reflecting this change with increased coverage of healthy practices such as meditation, positive attitudes, improved diet and exercise. As with most change, it will take time and patience, and we still have a long way to go.

Edgar Mitchell, the Apollo astronaut and IONS scientist, has not only been my science mentor, but I have helped him with his own health challenge using energy treatments. Because of Edgar's past personal experiences with cancer, as well as his work in the science of consciousness, he understands the concepts of energy healing. Says Mitchell, "The story of my life is an account of being hit on the head with astonishing experiences, which drove me to find an explanation."

Years before we met, Edgar Mitchell was healed energetically of prostate cancer. Then, a couple of years ago, he was diagnosed with a cancerous tumor in his kidney. Doctors wanted to operate, but instead of opting for surgery, he called me to see if I could help.

From 5000 miles away, I worked nonlocally with Edgar's holographic image, which I projected in front of me every two weeks, for six months. I found it very effective to imagine energetically wringing out the tumor in order to dry it out. I instructed Edgar to visualize drying out all of the vascular connections that this tumor had, effectively cutting off its survival capabilities. He did not undergo any other treatments, but simply continued with his healthy diet, exercise regimen and meditation. After one month, a CT scan showed that the size of the tumor was markedly reduced. Six months later, the growth had disappeared completely.

Edgar understands that we all possess our own healing abilities, making wellness our personal responsibility. This is the essence of self-empowerment. Working with a healer is always a participatory process, the healer a guide on a two-way street. Experience has previously shown Edgar that energy treatments work, so his beliefs and expectations were already in line with the treatment. As well, his body remembers how a successful outcome was achieved previously. Body memory or cell memory, as well as beliefs, influence outcome.

"We are simply blinded by the limitations of our current scientific paradigm," says the sixth man to walk on the moon.

"The most parsimonious explanation for my recovery is Adam's energy healing ability. Eventually we'll have a more complete scientific explanation of abilities such as Adam's (and our own)," Mitchell believes. "What we know so far about the subatomic realm and quantum holography is only the tip of the iceberg."

⸺

What do successful people from all disciplines have in common? They all have high self-expectations and a strong belief in themselves. They are visionaries, whether their vision is to win an Olympic gold medal or create a corporation. The belief in what they are setting out to accomplish is clear and unwavering. I have noticed that when it comes to their health challenges, they approach them with the same commitment. Belief and trust in themselves is reflected in the discipline and effectiveness of their healing visualizations.

It is often straightforward to positively influence sports injuries. I know that professional athletes could benefit tremendously by working with energy, as their careers depend on a speedy recovery. In recent years, sports psychology has played a major role in the success of many athletes. Many have come to understand the importance of visualizing what they want to achieve: They know what a powerful tool visualization is.

The media can also play a powerful role in shaping our society, including our beliefs. In the media's coverage of my treatment of Ronnie Hawkins, it brought the discussion of a less than mainstream topic to the fore. Rompin' Ronnie Hawkins has been described as the performer who brought rock and roll to Canada from his home state of Arkansas back in the 1950s. During his more than fifty years as a performer, he has met just about everyone in the music business. Outside Canada, he is best known for the major stars that performed with him. The backup group for Bob Dylan, The Band, was originally Ronnie's backing band and was later famous in its own right. In 1969, John Lennon and Yoko Ono stayed at Ronnie's place during their peace crusade.

A few years ago, I read an article in the local newspaper about Ronnie Hawkins and his battle with inoperable pancreatic cancer. He had gone in for surgery to remove the tumor the month before, but the doctors were unable to operate because the tumor was wrapped around an artery. According to the newspaper article, chemotherapy was not an option for Ronnie, and his cancer had been pronounced terminal. When I looked at his photograph in the paper, I thought that I could help. I contacted his manager, who responded that Ronnie was eager to try anything. He had never heard of distant healing but figured he had nothing to lose.

He said, "Five of the best doctors in the world have told me that this is it. They said three to six months, tops—I'm gone." His friends organized a private party in Ronnie's honor in Toronto, Canada. Many celebrities attended, including well-known Canadian music producer David Foster, former U.S. president

Bill Clinton, comedian Whoopi Goldberg, singer-composer Paul Anka, Ronnie's tycoon friend Don Tyson from Arkansas and Canadian industrialist Peter Pocklington. The evening was full of laughter and tears; Ronnie was very ill and was expected at most to live out only the rest of that year.

Two weeks later, in October, Ronnie was inducted into Canada's Walk of Fame. This ceremony is usually held in May, but he wasn't expected to live that long. Just a week before this, I had started distant treatments on Ronnie. Using a photograph, I energetically connected to him from 3000 miles away. Over the next six months, I did approximately sixty treatments with him. Ronnie was amazed to feel these treatments. He reported a fluttering feeling in his abdomen that persisted throughout the sessions.

Almost immediately, Ronnie's health began to improve. It was a surprise to everyone that he greeted in the new year. Even more wonderful was the news that his CT scan showed no evidence of any tumor remaining. An MRI a month and a half later confirmed that Ronnie was cancer-free. Now it is years later, and Ronnie continues to perform on stage and enjoy life.

Shortly after Ronnie was declared cancer-free, an article appeared in a popular American magazine. This piece produced an interesting yet unexpected effect. The magazine's target market is eighteen- to thirty-five-year-olds, younger than most people requesting treatments from me. Instead of health challenges, many of the readers were interested in how this information related to their own unusual experiences with energy. Some people who read the article had never heard the word "aura" before, yet they realized they had been seeing auras for years. Some saw colors; others had a feeling or just a sense of knowing. One woman reported that she always got information when she was physically close to others—for example, information about their moods and events that preceded their meeting. She was also able to help alleviate pain in others. When she confided in her mother, she was told to take a pill and lie down; her mom thought she must be ill. Others also reported that instead of receiving confirmation that their atypical experiences were real and worth exploring, their accounts were dismissed, which left them feeling confused. A number of readers reported being moved to tears as they recalled a meaningful personal experience that was disregarded or ignored.

It is always reassuring to people with unusual abilities to know that they are not alone. The magazine article gave many people permission to reveal their own experiences.

Children are keenly aware of reality beyond our five senses. It was wonderful to know that many young adults haven't forgotten what they once knew to be true. If these abilities are continually dismissed, their intensity often diminishes over time. Yet, with practice, one can revive these abilities. It is a matter of intention, learning to refocus and remembering what you have forgotten. Of course there is no age restriction on knowing that our abilities extend beyond our usual perception.

SPIRITUALITY

Spirituality is based on our intuitive knowing that there is more to our existence than what is dictated by our five senses of sight, hearing, taste, smell and touch. Merely inquiring as to what spirituality is suggests that you are spiritual. It is the act of contemplating our own existence. Since the beginning of time, humans have asked perplexing questions. Why are we here? What is our purpose? What is our role in this universe? Contemplating the meaning of life is in essence being spiritual. All organisms that are aware of their own existence are spiritual in some sense.

Our interconnectedness with everything in this universe plays a major role in defining our individual spirituality. How we view ourselves is not in isolation from everyone and everything else. The path each of us takes to understand our existence differs widely, but the search is nonetheless an integral part of our being. The spiritual search can be both personal and global. Our individual and collective quest to experience, express and explore the deeper meaning of knowledge and new ideas makes us spiritual. People vary greatly in their progress along a spiritual path. Some dedicate almost no time to understanding the universe; some devote their entire lives.

There is no limit to the number of questions that could arise as we ponder our role in the universe. I tend to take a scientific view on things, including life itself. What is the purpose of life? I personally do not like using the word "purpose" in this context because it implies that everything is predestined. I believe that life simply evolved in this vast amazing universe—from singularity to the incredibly complex world we experience today. All along there were unlimited probabilities, some of which manifested and some did not. We can't study the quantum world for long before coming face-to-face with mysteries of our seemingly nonphysical nature.

The scientific perspective on life is difficult for many people to accept. As conscious entities, our wish is not only to understand the universe—an exciting, never-ending quest—but to find meaning. The connectedness that quantum physicists describe has a meaningful aspect. This interconnection between each of our individual consciousnesses is something so complex that striving to understand it is a productive and fulfilling objective. There will always be something yet to be explored or beyond our understanding, and the human appetite to pursue answers cannot be ignored. Science is one of our best tools to use in this pursuit.

Many people feel that religion answers the question of how we came to be. There are many religions in the world today, and each follower believes that his or her religion is the true religion. Spirituality is definitely a part of religion, but one does not have to be religious to be spiritual. Religion is an organized group activity, while spirituality is an individual knowingness emanating from within. Belief in God or Allah or Jehovah then becomes a matter of individual faith and experience.

Other belief systems not recognized as organized religions also embrace a spiritual way of life. North American Native cultures have always had a great respect for the spiritual world. These beliefs provide them with their direction and timing for action and reflection. Their culture speaks of many guides, which are evident in their practices and customs. Totem poles are an artistic representation of important cultural information, such as clans, spirit guides and significant events, representing a set of beliefs at a particular time. These images include many of animals that act as messengers to guide them.

North American Native nations understand that individual contentment is based on the collective needs of all. This belief underlies everything they do in their daily activities and ensures harmony within their culture. Their philosophy of cooperation rather than competition was foreign to the Europeans who took over the Native land and tried to dominate their cultures. When the Europeans came to North America, they outlawed the spiritual beliefs of the Natives. Yet, what was seen by the Europeans as a primitive and regressive culture is actually the direction in which we all must move to achieve global sustainability.

Many wars throughout civilization have been based on misguided religious beliefs. The message that can unite all religions is: We are all one. Since we are all connected to the same field of information, ideally we would all have a unified understanding about consciousness and spirituality. Can you imagine the peace in the world if all religions started preaching from the same page? This is the unification that is required for our world to survive.

It is of the greatest importance to be open to learning and not get bogged down with dogmatism that divides us and stifles our progress. Your beliefs are ultimately a personal and private matter. Whether you define yourself as Christian, Jew, Hindu, Buddhist, Muslim, agnostic, atheist or what have you, the important thing is that we all embrace our differences and accept one another.

I see the difference between various religious philosophies as primarily a matter of semantics. The quantum physics term "energy field" is interchangeable with "the divine power of a deity." I generally avoid religious and cultural terms and prefer to speak from a scientific perspective. Scientific terminology is inclusive of everyone, rather than exclusive to only those of a particular cultural heritage or religious belief. Balancing of spiritual thoughts and ideas to form a collective consciousness for all of humankind should be everyone's goal. A unified approach would view "God" (or "Allah," or "Jehovah," and so on) as a different name for the same thing: the One Mind; the collective consciousness or energy source. The collective consciousness of all organisms in the universe has a tendency to influence events in various ways. Our overall goal should be to understand these interconnections of consciousness that we share with each other and everything else in the universe for the greater good of all.

Spirituality is based on our intuitive feeling of knowing that there are more subtleties to our existence than are picked up by the five senses. We must respect life by being aware. Sometimes life is to be heard, at other times it is to be seen and, almost always, it is to be felt. Our inner knowing will guide us. By becoming more aware, we move toward understanding ourselves. Through a better understanding of ourselves, we become more accepting of the harmony required for all of us to benefit from each other within a cooperative system.

Spirituality is ultimately a deep belief within yourself; it is the basis of your belief system and includes what you desire, expect and know will happen. Connecting to your own spirituality will allow you to move forward and achieve anything you can imagine. When you understand the origin of your thoughts, you are more in tune with yourself in every thought, word and action. Clarity of awareness is available to us to interpret every experience so that we can go forward with confidence. We can then embrace every new situation and challenge. This is the key to happiness.

Many of our spiritual beliefs lie in our subconscious minds. By uniting our subconscious beliefs and conscious intentions, we truly awaken our spirituality. We can then synchronize our thoughts, intentions and actions.

How does suffering—particularly, suffering from an illness— relate to spirituality? On an individual level, physical suffering can serve as a pivotal point in our lives: It is often a powerful wake-up call demanding our immediate attention. View this as a chance to take control of your health, reflect upon your life and notice where you are heading. In the long run, such suffering may force the development of self-responsibility and self-empowerment. Recognition of spiritual issues is part and parcel of this development.

In a more global view, when someone suffers, we all suffer, because we are all connected. Of course, those people closest to that person feel the most pain from their loved one's suffering.

As our global community shrinks, we increasingly find that people of every religion are becoming our neighbors, friends and relatives. Religion is a particular set of answers, within a historical and cultural context, to the spiritual questions people pose. We must learn to embrace the differences in interpretation since ultimately what is similar in each religion is the principle of love and acceptance. Our growing connections will help rid us of intolerance—an essential step in the survival of humankind. Our increasing global consciousness reflects the interconnectedness that we all share and is the basis of the ongoing paradigm shift in our thinking.

Sometimes a person might not get well because it is their time to move on—it is their time to die. You have said that you often intuitively pick up this information. Since beliefs play such a major role in our well-being, how do you handle that?

I believe that it is not something I should tell a person. I am not always right. Even if I were, it would not be appropriate to share any information that might influence a person's beliefs and their intention to get well.

How many treatments do people typically require? Does it depend on the person's belief system?

The number of treatments depends primarily on the illness, though the manipulation of energy in the body can be enhanced or slowed by the healee's specific beliefs. Many illnesses can be helped significantly with only a few treatments—joint pain, lower back pain, migraines and asthma among them. Even though some of these health challenges have been with a person for decades, they can sometimes be relieved in just a few treatments. Other illnesses, such as cancer, may require many treatments. This is why it is imperative that people understand what they can do for themselves. As in so many aspects of life, you can always count on yourself.

Have you ever worked with someone you couldn't help?

Most people I work with notice a difference, and if they stay with the treatments, they usually improve. About 90 percent of those I work with notice sensations during treatments.

Some people are curious to try energy healing but find it difficult to get their heads around it. Indeed, some may begin to follow the exercises in this book but be unable to keep with it. Energy healing is participatory and requires clear motivation and persistent practice on the part of the healee. Any conflicting beliefs that a person has may impede the journey to wellness. That is, the person may consciously want to get well but is unconsciously blocking the healing process.

Chapter 8

Reincarnation

Reincarnation allows for the ultimate learning curve in the progress of all things.

—ADAM

$\mathcal{R}$eincarnation is the mechanism for the transmission of information from one lifetime to the next. It is the process of repeated rebirth in a never-ending cycle of birth, life and death. I have some memories of past lives. Most are fragmented, but some are quite clear and some are traumatic.

Hundreds of years ago, I was a member of a Native American tribe. My home was surrounded by grassy hills, and a river flowed nearby. Life was peaceful. One day, a scout returned home with disturbing news. He had witnessed the decimation of a neighboring tribe, and the killers were headed toward our village. Immediately, a meeting was called. The elder medicine man told us that twelve men would stay behind to defend the village. Everyone else was to leave at once and get as far away as possible.

Within minutes, the women, children and many of the men left. My younger brother and I remained behind with ten other men. That was when the shaman said that he saw our main purpose in staying behind as giving the others a head start, thereby escaping the impending attack. He also revealed that all twelve men who stayed behind would be killed defending our village. Many years before this, when I was young, he had told me that my brother and I would die together.

That night as we gathered around the fire, no one spoke. Each of us gazed silently into the flames, absorbed by our own thoughts. Just after sunrise, we were attacked by several men from another tribe. They were accompanied by white men. One of the white men pointed a stick at me. I charged at him with my mallet-like weapon. As I reached him, I realized that I was bleeding. I hadn't recognized his stick as a gun, since I had never seen a gun before: I had no way of knowing that I had been shot.

As I dropped to the ground holding my chest, my head turned to the side. I found myself gazing directly into the eyes of my brother, who lay only a few feet away. He was pinned to the ground by the attackers and being scalped alive. He saw me and our eyes locked. The look of terror in his eyes ripped through me. There was nothing I could do to help my little brother; I was dying too. So I smiled at him. That was all I could give him: a smile.

It is still an emotional experience for me to recall this life. Because of this, I understand the impact that memories can have on people. Some people have vivid memories of past life experiences, others remember fragments and many people have no recollection at all. Regardless of what we do or don't remember, our past lives have an impact on our emotional and thus physical health.

Reincarnation is a natural process, one of the everyday events in the universe. A scientific definition of reincarnation would draw on theories derived from our current body of knowledge of physics, especially of how energy behaves in our universe. One of the laws of physics is that energy can be neither created nor destroyed. Reincarnation, which involves a person's energy essence being passed on from one lifetime to another, is no exception to this rule: One's composite of energy (light) frequencies does not cease at the time of death but transfers to the next life.

Reincarnation is not all that mysterious in the context of the subtle energies and light emissions that I have been discussing. As I described earlier, each of us has a unique frequency connection to the universal field of information; this is our signature link to everything at any time, and our eternal energy essence. This energy essence is referred to as the soul in many religions. It is all the information from all your previous lives—the unique way in which light has coordinated all of your cells throughout all of your incarnations. This is who you are. The cumulative light frequency emitted from a multi-cellular organism (such as a human being or animal) coordinates and unifies all of the cells within it into one harmonious organism. At the time of physical death, this unifying frequency of light goes through a transformation process as it becomes the essence of life in a new organism.

Reincarnation, as a means to preserve energy essence, is essential for human evolution, as well as for all other creatures great and small. It allows for the ultimate learning experience in the progression of all things.

Every living organism has a focal point of light emissions. This point is the center of information exchange and is where the light emitted within the body is at the greatest concentration. When I connect to someone's hologram, this focal point appears to me as a bright white light near the center of the brain. It is from here that we tune in to the field of information.

In life, the body is always in a dynamic state of disequilibria in terms of biophoton emissions and biochemical reactions. The constant state of rebalancing, or flux, is the state of disequilibria. In life, our energy is never totally balanced. Life is a constant balance and counterbalance process between emissions and reactions. At the point of death, the body reaches a state of equilibrium. A balance is finally achieved. The light frequency—the energy essence—dissipates, and then eventually manifests in the new organism, identical to what it was in the previous form.

One's state of mind and intentions at the moment of death have a great influence on what will occur as one passes from one physical life to the next. Your characteristics throughout your life—what you are like, the kinds of thought patterns that you typically have—will influence the pattern of your energy essence in your next life. The thoughts, both conscious and subconscious, that you have at the time of death play a large part in determining your next incarnate, or bodily, form. Those thoughts, of course, are usually in sync with your typical personality patterns.

Generally, if you had good thoughts and intentions throughout your life, these would be on your mind at the point of departure, or death. It's possible that someone who has lived an exemplary life is not connecting to positive intentions at the moment of death. Conversely, another person might have lived his or her life as an angry, self-centered person but managed at this transitional time to emanate positive thoughts and intentions. Although it is possible to change your focus toward the end of life, it is much easier to transfer a well-established path. It is a lot more work to instantly forge a new one.

Where your intention is focused at the exact moment of death determines the direction your new life will take. Your thoughts emit a particular energy frequency that links to and affects everything else. This influences the exchange of information at that time. If your thinking and intentions are vague and unfocused, your successive incarnate body will be selected as randomly as your thoughts are random. If you are thinking with clear, focused intention, you are more likely to influence what occurs. Your thoughts at the time of death are affected by the circumstances of your death. A violent, emotional or painful death would have a different influence than a peaceful parting in your sleep.

Our intentions are like a compass needle in the sense that they direct our energy through this transfer. Where the compass is pointing at the time of death guides us. We can influence this through our choices. Intention affects everything much more than we may be aware. It is important to understand how essential self-reflection and self-assessment are in maximizing our influence on our destinies. Your intention is the main guiding process in the transition from one life to the next. Of course, many factors line up at the time of death to pave the path of transition, the path to the next life: The outcome is a result of the sum of all of the smaller influences and experiences of your life journey too.

It is important, at the time of death, to reflect on what your intentions are and what you want to happen. It all comes down to intention. What messages are you sending out to the field? By aligning your conscious and subconscious thoughts, dealing with emotional and psychological baggage and thus lessening the impact of it on your daily life, and giving yourself daily affirmations, you can learn to focus your intention.

Your consciousness, present in every atom and cell, also exists externally of your physical self. Your own consciousness, rather than some external force, guides your new life and your new incarnation. The power to be your own guide lies totally within yourself.

Your combination of attitudes and degree of awareness puts you at a certain vibration level, and you will resonate with or be influenced more by the consciousness, or energy, of others at a similar vibration level. You are also affected by the collective consciousness, though not to a degree that redirects your own intention.

Many of us have been intrigued by accounts of near-death experiences. They almost always involve an intense, bright light and sometimes feelings of warmth more powerful than the sun. People report intense emotions such as overwhelming love, happiness, joy and contentment. Their entire lives replay before them in their mind's eye—every thought, word and deed. Feelings of peace and calm often linger with the person long after the experience.

These accounts by adults and children alike are consistent throughout history, transcending culture and religion. An out-of-body experience is felt as a spiritual conscious awareness such as we all will experience during the process of death and reincarnation. The difference, of course, is that in a near-death experience, death does not occur, so the person regains consciousness in the same physical self. The process of transformation is incomplete. In the process of reincarnation, on the other hand, there is a point of no return, when our connection to memories in the field is shifted from the conscious and subconscious level of self to the subconscious of the new self.

Based on the reports of people who have had a near-death experience, at the point of death, we experience an intense light. Some people report seeing this light, others feel it. This bright light imprints all data contained within us at our particular frequency or vibration—our signature. Next we go through what appears to be a tunnel as we experience an overwhelming sense of interconnectedness to everyone and everything else in the universe, and therefore the field. Accompanying this feeling of being a part of everything is our knowing that we are not separate consciousnesses. We are truly a collective consciousness.

One's new physical body is imprinted with the information that contains all of the data from all of one's past lives. As I discuss above, the connection between this information in the old body and the new incarnate is directed, through intentions and thoughts at the moment of death, by the person's unique frequency.

To appreciate the process of reincarnation, it is essential to understand the pivotal role energy and light frequencies play in human reproduction. The energy of the egg is different from the energy of the mother. The egg alone doesn't yet have the life force, which is the light that binds the cells together. At the moment of conception, when the energies of the egg and sperm merge, the newly created entity acquires the life (light) force. This signature frequency of light information starts to influence an embryo, coordinating the development of the new organism. Consciousness reemerges in this new form.

In this way, our connection to all information in the field is complete, and our biophoton emissions light up with the light of life. Light emanates from every cell and an aura appears around the new body as the energy of all cells starts coordinating the cells' functions in synchronicity with the frequency. This energetic self is the essence of life. It is this that lives on, reconnecting to a new body during the process of reincarnation.

Death is an inevitable part of the reincarnation process. I haven't witnessed a person dying, but I witnessed the death of our cat and the energetic process of death must be the same, as cats and humans are both multi-cellular organisms. When our cat was euthanized at twenty-one years of age, I stared into her eyes the entire time she was dying. As she died, the harmonious flow of her aura became fragmented. All of the brilliant colors began to fade to grayish tones. Then a static-like pattern emerged as the speed of the aura's motion gradually slowed. After about half an hour, her aura was completely gray and almost stagnant. I kept my thoughts on what a wonderful friend she had been to me all of my life, knowing that this would influence her last thoughts and impressions in this life. Her new incarnate will receive guidance and direction from this in the same way that it does with humans.

The question of how long we remain between incarnations without a physical body has no real meaning when we are out-of-body. In that state, we are no longer restricted by space and time limitations. We are only energy as information, as we always have been. Our illusion of physical self provided us with rules that no longer apply. At death, our energy is in the form of waves, which do not operate as a function of time in the way energy does when it is particles of matter.

Once again, each of us has the ability to influence our incarnate selection as we manipulate our own energy through thoughts and intentions while we are alive. What we can accomplish in one life is a continuation of what we can accomplish in the next. We learn and we continue to learn.

If there is any reckoning that we must face, it is that which we arrive at through self-reflection of our thoughts, words, actions and intentions. Only we know our every thought and deed during our lifetime. Only we can visualize what impact our lives have had on anything and therefore everything else. We must stand before ourselves and review what we have done. This should not be thought of in a judgmental way, as it is an extension of our lifetime learning process. Any lessons that we need to address become clear to us upon self-reflection. This is the same self-reflection process that you have used to access your own self-talk and beliefs.

Our memories in this life cease at the point of death. A shift takes place, which transforms the connection of all memories in the field into the subconscious of the new body. The energy that is reincarnated is specific and, in that sense, our connection to the field remains identical. When this frequency connects to the new body, however, change inevitably starts to occur with every experience of the new environment. Once our conscious awareness returns to a new physical form, these various experiences start to shape our perception of events. Your subconscious self, the repository of your energy essence, is the accumulation of your many lifetimes. You are, in effect, the sum of many existences.

Two perspectives are joined with each reincarnation: the person in the previous life and the person in the new life. From the perspective of the person in the previous life, everything ends at the point of death. The energy information transfer from the old body to the new is beyond conscious awareness. However, the memories of the past life are continuous in the new life whether the "new" you is consciously aware of them or not. These memories resonate within every cell of your being, since your unique connection to the field of all information is ubiquitous—that is, everywhere at the same time. Reincarnation allows us to accumulate the wisdom and understanding to choose wisely through our developing spirits. This is spiritual evolution. Ultimately, a greater understanding of this process should lead to a deeper appreciation of all of humanity.

We can influence who, what, where and when our next life will be through focused intention. We can choose with whom we share the closest relationships, what we want and need to learn and what we can contribute toward the collective good. Your intentions have a much greater effect than you may be aware. Choose your wishes wisely.

How and when does the holographic information from a former body imprint on the new incarnate? How and when does this information get transferred?

I'm not exactly sure. It might be at the point of conception because that is when the biophoton emissions start coordinating the development of cells. Those cells are who you are—what is unique to you. The way in which light emissions are organizing your cells is what constitutes your mind—your consciousness. As soon as light begins coordinating the formation of cells, consciousness is present. What comes with that consciousness is all information from all previous lives.

What form do we take after dying and leaving the body behind?

We become a different form of energy—or what I call a wave function. That is what you are—a wave function, whether you are in a physical body or not. Without a physical body, you will be absorbed into the field and will continue to have energy properties. You may not consciously be aware of where you are or what's happening, but your intentions will still influence things.

Can an animal reincarnate as another type of animal—as a human, for example?

Yes. For example, in the case of my cat, the vast majority of her memories are of people. Her intentions throughout her life and at the time of her death are going to be focused on people because she was around people all of her life. If her intentions were constantly on people, the chance of her coming back as a human is high. The intentions of both humans and animals at the time of death are a main factor in what form the incarnation will take.

Chapter 9
Karma

Our reality is influenced, but not determined, by karma.

—ADAM

I am often asked at my workshops about karma—the nature and influence of the energy that is transferred from one incarnation to the next—and its relationship to illness. Health and healing is part of who we are and who we have been. For instance, I have had a health issue revisit me from the past.

Several years ago, I was one of the healers invited to the First Nations International Healing and Medicines Gathering held at the Nekaneet First Nation in Saskatchewan. The setting is the beautiful grasslands where Cree people have lived for centuries. It was an honor to take part in the traditional Native ceremonies and to work with shamans from around the globe.

During the entire week of the Gathering, there was always a long lineup of people outside one particular shaman's teepee of the ten that made up the healing circle. When I arrived at my teepee each morning, people were already lined up outside that teepee. When I left in the evening, a lengthy line remained. I wasn't able to catch even a glimpse of the shaman, as he never left his teepee, choosing to eat and sleep there too.

After the closing ceremonies, I was packing my belongings when a man approached me. He introduced himself as the assistant to that shaman. The aide said that the shaman would like to meet me now if it was convenient. My mom also wanted to meet the shaman, so we went together to his teepee.

The shaman and I recognized each other immediately and we spoke, in telepathic images, of knowing each other in a past life. He and I had been close in a previous life. We were in the same tribe, I being the older of the two of us. He remembered us both being on horseback and my being shot in my right shoulder with an arrow. Telepathically through images, he asked how my shoulder was. I rolled up my sleeve and showed him a scar on my right shoulder.

The past life shoulder trauma seems to have followed me into this lifetime, because when I was thirteen years old in my current life, I injured my right shoulder in a bus accident and had to have surgery on it. There would have been a number of ways for me to break my fall as the bus driver slammed on the brakes, but it was my shoulder that took the brunt of the impact. This doesn't necessarily mean that the shoulder injury in my current life was a certainty. It was not inevitable or unpreventable. Karma does not directly cause things to happen. Rather, the tendency or likelihood of an event is present as a karmic influence: Karma influences events to occur in a particular manner or sequence. My shoulder injury wasn't directly caused by the karmic influence, but that influence did play a role in my breaking my fall with my shoulder. My reaction may have been in my subconscious when I reacted to the event.

After a brief conversation, the shaman and I parted, as there was still a lineup of people outside his teepee waiting to see him. I am sure our paths will cross again.

Karma is commonly thought of as the baggage that we carry with us from one life to the next. However, once again, a law of physics provides us with a more accurate perspective on karma: For every action, there is an equal and opposite reaction. This suggests that energy seeks equilibrium. Some people take this law and apply moral considerations to it, calling it karma. For example, a common belief is that if you have evil intentions in one life, your karma will be to make restitution in the next, thereby balancing out good and evil or achieving equilibrium.

It seems to me that some people underestimate the role of karma in events and others overestimate it, by claiming that unfortunate events are due to karma. Karma plays a subtle role in our everyday lives. It is not operating to punish you for actions in a past life. I understand karma to be less rigid than a system of restitution, and not predestined. It is just energy—and, remember, there is no good or bad energy; energy is just energy—that works and moves in various ways according to natural laws. And karma is not limited to humans but applies to all living organisms.

Offspring can be influenced by their parents' karma—but in an environmental sense rather than a genetic sense. In the womb, the baby is growing and developing, surrounded by the mother's energy. The mother's energy is like a conductor of electricity. The fetus attracts the mother's energy but has its own energy patterns. Yet, it generally moves energy in a similar fashion to that of the mother and so experiences a similar flow.

As I discussed earlier, every organism emits a unique frequency of light that connects to the field of information. This connection can increase the likelihood of certain events occurring. These frequencies of light emitted from your body can influence events in subtle ways, which cumulatively can influence larger events that may seem unrelated.

For instance, if you are angry all the time, you will outwardly demonstrate this emotion, and your frequency will closely correlate with that of anger. The events that occur around you will thrive in an environment of anger. Certain events will be more probable, such as conflict with another person, leading to a chain of events that makes you think that you have bad karma. What is actually happening is that your angry attitude is attracting more anger. What you refer to as your karma is the result of your habitual thoughts and intentions.

As one's essence reincarnates, some similar traits or inclinations from a previous life tend to carry over to the next; that, too, is karma. Those inclinations, in turn, will affect the events that may happen in your new life. So a person's energy essence, you might say, while not identical to that in a previous life, has some similarity. There are always differences; things are constantly changing. Each life is a new beginning. Remember that when you reincarnate, your new body is in another time and often a different place, which means new experiences. You will have a different genetic makeup and be raised in a different environment. These influences can mitigate karma. Environment plays a more influential role in our lives than does genetics. Certain environments allow specific energies to thrive and others to be less important. If you are raised in an environment that encourages growth, then growth characterizes your thoughts and intentions and you will progress accordingly. Conversely, if you have to cope in a fear-based environment, that negative conditioning will become a particular challenge to overcome. This is why karma can only be an influence, and not a certainty. Nothing is predetermined.

We choose our own paths; free will guides our journeys. Our subconscious memories from previous lives and the similar frequency from one life to another do have an impact. But we can look at these tendencies as challenges to overcome. We create our own destiny: Karma is only an influence on events. Within our new selves, we can intend and create new possibilities to positively influence any existing karmic patterns. There is always the choice—and hence the potential—to wipe the slate clean. We can consciously choose how we are going to react to any karmic influences, subconscious programming and the environment in which we find ourselves.

There is no karmic law that you must relive all of the bad and ugly events of past lives, even if you vividly remember some events and experiences in this life. But past life memories can be traumatic. This is because the most vivid memories often occur at transition, or the moment of death, as we have the clearest recollection of our most emotionally charged events. Those moments where intense emotions intertwine with memory give us recall of the experience. Memories from past lives are usually subconscious feelings triggered by events in the present life.

Every one of us gets impressions or feelings about past, present or future events. People react to such sensations differently. Many people rely heavily on their gut instincts. Others try hard to dismiss these signals that their subconscious is sending them.

I am often able to pick up images from a person's past lives. Generally, the images are brief and random. Sometimes they make a lot of sense to the person when I relate them, and other times not. The images won't resonate with the person unless he or she has experienced a meaningful event connecting this subconscious information from a past life to events in the current life.

To access past life information, I connect to the person the same way as I would if doing a treatment. I then access the center of the brain, where there is the highest concentration of light and therefore the highest concentration of information. It is here that I receive information about past lives.

One woman I met wanted to know what I could see of her past lives. When I did a reading on her, I telepathically received two brief images. In the first image, she was descending a staircase, lit by a torch, to a dungeon; the next image was of prison bars. These images made perfect sense to her when I told her of them. Many years earlier, she was touring in Europe. As she approached a castle, she became nauseated and fearful. She refused to go inside and skipped the tour. At the time, she could not explain this reaction, but she felt strongly that she could not enter the castle—and she followed her feelings. My past life reading therefore immediately resonated with her. If we can understand what triggers our fears and negative emotions, we can control our reactions to them. It is possible to reestablish all of the positive learning experiences while repatterning the negative ones. Again, there is no karmic law that you must relive all of the bad and ugly events, so only keep what you need for self-enlightenment.

Living life with a positive outlook and expecting positive outcomes is important for achieving your goal. Your intentions must be clearly focused on what you want and expect to happen. If good health is your objective, be clear in your intention. Positively influence any karmic patterns with your intentions. By doing the exercises in this book, you will align your conscious and subconscious thoughts, effectively adjust emotional reactions to be more favorable and be able to focus on what you want through affirmations. Emphasize what you want to achieve in order for the best possibilities to manifest themselves.

Our seeking a purpose for the existence of karma is a very human activity, one growing out of the desire for meaning in life. The transfer of energy from one life to the next is a natural evolution. Since energy cannot be destroyed, it transmutes into another life.

From an evolutionary perspective, karma is one of many variables that influence the energetic aspect of the self as it continues from one lifetime to the next. Another variable is how quickly you reincarnate to another life—the physical transition is not necessarily instantaneous. Another influence on our energetic self is the thoughts and intentions that are in your mind when you die, as discussed in the previous chapter on reincarnation. Of course, you are influenced by the body you are going into and the who, what and where circumstances of your new incarnate. For example, the challenges of a prince are different than those of a pauper. Everything changes somewhat: your personality, the environment that influences you, your appearance. The process is dynamic. You are always evolving, from one incarnation to the next, just as you evolve and make changes within each lifetime, which is itself the sum of all of your incarnations.

What is relatively stable is the manner in which light coordinates your cells—the frequency of that light remains somewhat the same. As I discuss in the previous chapter, this is the essence or soul of a person. So, from lifetime to lifetime, certain patterns will be similar. But if the incarnate does not encounter a challenge from a previous life because of entirely different circumstances in the new life, karma may not be much of an influence.

Often a variety of small effects—small changes—cause a series of events to occur, which can result in interesting coincidences between different lifetimes. One of my mom's past lives illustrates this point. In that past life, she was a nun in a clinic, dedicated to helping and healing people. She had been born into a poverty-stricken family and had many siblings. When she became an adult, she had the choice of getting married into equally abject poverty and repeating the cycle, or becoming a nun. She chose the latter because it offered more possibilities. Her empathy for others led her to start a clinic dedicated to healing. I intuitively knew that my mother would recognize the way she referred to the work she did in her clinic in her past life—as healing "hearts, minds and souls." When I told her about this during a past life reading, she shivered; the recollection of this past life resonated with her. She now finds herself helping others in this lifetime as well, by helping me with my healing workshops.

We are in control of pointing our own compasses—another way of describing free will. At first it might seem that karma and free will are contradictory concepts. But this is not so: Your free will has determined your karmic influences. Your choices have all been of your own free will. We are constantly making choices—every minute of every day. Our environment influences the choice we make, but we are always the driving force; the chosen route is not externally imposed upon us. When we change our minds about something, karmic influences are changed accordingly. Nothing is written in stone, so to speak. As I've said before, energy is a neutral force that behaves according to how we direct it. One obvious characteristic of the universe and evolution is constant change. We exist in a dynamic system.

I have been asked whether karma affects thoughts as well as actions. There is no distinction between an action and a thought in terms of karma. A thought has a particular energy, which initiates its link to everything. An action also links to and has an effect on the energetic flow, thereby setting a certain chain of events into motion. The only difference between the two is that an action alters the awareness and reactions of others. In a dominolike effect, others see the action and their collective attention amplifies the energetic effect of that action.

Many people believe that the root cause of an illness can be traced to an incident from a past life. In my view, there is no illness that karma or a past life event is solely responsible for. Nobody deserves to be ill. Some people take some comfort in the concept of karma as a reason for their illness. They say that it is a lesson that must be learned from a past life. This is not a productive outlook for anyone embarking on a healing journey through self-empowerment. A healthier perspective is to put all past events aside and travel forward on the path of healing. Simply consider the lesson as having been learned and that it is now time to get better. Take responsibility for your way forward in thought, word and action. Start making changes from within.

In no circumstances should you play the role of the victim. Life is as dynamic as you are. Make the changes that will be beneficial to you on your health and healing journey. Be flexible. Make sure that you are ready, willing and able to accept change. We must focus on re-creating what we want to achieve. Always see the glass as being half full rather than half empty. Imprint this attitude into your being until it is ingrained within everything you think, say and do. Give credit where credit is due when good things are achieved, especially if it is your own accomplishment. Sometimes it may seem impossible to reach your goals, but two steps forward and one step back is still progress in the direction you want.

Life is for learning. Regain your footing. Blaming an illness on past lives and karma is not productive. In our current life, we *can* directly influence events and carry on. Failure occurs only by not trying in the first place. Establish your goal and make it happen.

You mention that the role of karma on events is sometimes overemphasized. Why is this a concern?

Each time you reincarnate, you start with a new environment and a new body. Your intentions may change with the new incarnate, thus influencing your energy. You can always change your present intentions and influence your present health. I'm concerned that if people feel that their illness involves a lesson to be learned, they might tend to accept it as fate rather than changing it. Life is a dynamic experience; it is not predetermined. It's important not to use karma as an excuse to be sick, as this will undermine your intention and determination to get well.

How have your past lives been revealed to you—through dreams, waking memories, visions?

Some have come to me in dreams, some in visions and some occur when I go to certain places—I just know I've been there before and I recognize specific locations and recall events. Often these past life memories are as clear to me as my childhood memories from this life.

Chapter 10
The Spirit World

After physical death, the essence of life exists without physical form until it unites with a new incarnate.

—ADAM

*A*t my workshops I meet many people who feel strongly connected to spirits and the spirit world. This issue weighs heavily on their minds, as our society is reluctant to address such issues as valid ones. Yet anything that concerns us spiritually influences our physical and psychological health and wellness. In this way, the spirit world is inseparable from our health and healing. How we view life after death most certainly influences our lives. Culture plays a dominant role in our views about the spirit world, as does religion and our own experiences throughout our lifetimes.

Many people are sensitive to our energetic connections. At my workshops, I am often asked whether I see spirits—what some people refer to as ghosts. In response, I sometimes relate this story about one encounter I had with a spirit.

I was on a canoe trip with my parents along a river that snaked through the mountains. While heading up the river, I became aware of a spirit trying to get my attention. To me, spirits look like an aura without a physical body. As I had encountered them many times before, I was curious, but not afraid. This spirit followed us along the shoreline, in the thick bushes. As we paddled, it sent me a message. Several minutes later, I asked my parents that we pull over, and so we stopped on a stretch of beach. I felt compelled go into the bush and connect with this spirit.

When I emerged from the bush, my dad said I looked like I had seen a ghost. I told him that the spirit was of an old Native elder. The information this spirit shared with me was about the massacre of his friends and family, including him. When I connected to this spirit, I received vivid images of the massacre. I could see Natives being scalped and murdered with axes and knives. For me, it was an intense experience to relive, in a sense, his experience. I could telepathically see this event from his perspective as his story in images repeatedly replayed. It was like watching a movie in which the elder's last intention as one of the murder victims was the storyline. His intent was to tell someone what happened and not let the murderers get away with the crime.

The spirit told me to "go where the eyes look." At first I didn't know what this meant. Then I intuitively knew to look up over my right shoulder at the mountain behind me. I found myself staring up at a steep, heavily forested mountain. The mouths of two caves near the top looked like large eyes in the mountainside. The spirit had instructed me to "go where the eyes look," so I allowed my gaze to follow the line of sight of the "eyes" in the mountainside. From where my parents and I stood, they appeared to be looking at a spot on another densely forested mountain. The hike to that mountain looked like an extremely difficult one. Since I believed the spirit's story about the massacre, I felt it was not necessary to go to the spot itself.

This fragmented piece of information appeared to me in images that repeated like a movie running in a loop. It was this elder's emotionally charged intent to have someone verify what was done to him and his family. Since time is of no relevance in the spirit world, he would have no inkling of the time that had passed. Of course, from our perspective, the lapse of time has made punishment, retribution or justice for the massacre by legal means unfeasible. I believe that what connected his energy to mine was not only my ability to tune in to such fragments but a resonance that exists with my Native ancestry. But there are many other factors to this connection, including the intense emotion that the elder felt during this event at his life's end.

When discussing the spirit world, it is important to remember that all of the information in the universe is within the field. This means that nonphysical fragments—those fragments that were once part of the energy systems of living organisms (that is, previous entities) but are no longer part of any organism—can be accessed. The host organism has died and reincarnated, but some residual information was not attached in the process. A fragment of data was left behind, so to speak. Although this fragment will eventually dissipate and be absorbed into the field, it stays together as a unified fragment for an undetermined length of time. I do receive information as it gets bounced off such fragments.

Sometimes what remains after death is a very large fragment, which can appear in the general shape of a human. This is what most people mean when they speak of spirits or ghosts. These fragments of information may seem to have some awareness as they go about their activities; they may carry a sufficient amount of information from when they were in material form that makes them appear to function like a person still. For instance, they may be engaged in activities such as walking or talking. However, most of the time they appear to me as just a repetitive loop of data on a seemingly endless replay, which represents the fragment of information left behind. This energy fragment is usually of a very emotional event that occurred in the last life. One way to think of spirits is as being similar to an audio recording of someone's voice. Even though the person might be long dead, the taped voice remains and can be replayed over and over.

People who interpret fragments as actual personalities of deceased individuals—or angels—may be overstating the role of fragments. I think that rather than these spirit fragments helping or protecting us, they exist merely as information remaining from their former life.

Nevertheless, even a fragment of information can have some influence on us, since any intention of any sort affects everything else. A fragment may have a connection to a person; for instance, Native spirits have an affinity to connect with me, likely because of my Native heritage. Because of that attachment, the spirit will naturally tend to exert an influence, just to keep that connection. There are many ways a person could have a connection to one of these fragments. Your simple thought or intention could be similar to the thought or intention of that spirit at that time. This creates a momentary connection, sometimes enough for the spirit to turn its attention to you. That is an automatic, natural process. So, fragments have an influence as part of a chain of events, but not a direct influence. Many fragments have no influence at all.

If you feel that your life is disrupted by a ghost, what you may actually be aware of is a fragment of information that does not have consciousness. No matter how we perceive spirits, we have to recognize that we are all connected to this spirit information. In most cases, we pass spirits off as nothing and ignore them. Once a person becomes more aware of these connections, he or she will be more influenced by them.

Not everything or everyone who dies leaves information behind in this form. A fragment has a frequency—it is a vibrational entity just like everything else. When you die, your intentions at the time of death will determine whether any of your memory gets "stuck" in this frequency, in the sense that a piece of your memory remains in nonphysical form in this reality. That is, your intention may be to leave this reality, but your frequency might be a little off. As a result, there will be pieces of your information that are misdirected in the process and left behind. A fragment is left to influence our physical world in this reality for a time.

After death, a person is in spirit form—that is, in waves rather than particles. From the perspective of our physical selves in our day-to-day lives, time is very important. For example, it takes time to get from point A to point B. From the perspective of the spirit, which exists as a wave, the time it takes to make a connection or have an influence has no real meaning; time is irrelevant. The instant that you die you are in spirit form, or waves. If your intention—conscious or subconscious—at the time of your death worked, it has manifested.

Some people refer to spirits as beings from another dimension but, in my opinion, "dimension" is not the right word to use. These fragments occur within our reality of space-time. It is misleading to divide our universe into dimensions. We do this for our own convenience, as many concepts involving energy, time and space are very difficult to define. There are, however, an infinite number of multiple subsets of information that may be overlapping.

A fragment of information, or spirit entity, can be seen by people who are tuned to its visual frequency. Large spirit fragments are found in many places. I have seen them in graveyards, shopping malls, tennis courts and in the wilderness. To me, they look like auras, except with no energetic flow and without the physical host. In other words, I see an aura without a body. This is more likely to be the case if the fragment is from someone who died traumatically, as the imprint is emotional.

How do fragments differ from each other?

Some are more complex pieces of information than others. Some will have the vague appearance of a body and even appear to be engaged in an activity, such as walking.

What are spirits?

Spirits are simply pieces of information. They are not conscious entities deliberately trying to frighten us. Some people have told me that they have encountered spirits that are able to make noise or move objects. It could be that an information fragment is complex enough to manipulate matter in some way. I haven't seen this, but theoretically it is possible.

Can we influence these fragments with our intentions?

Yes, theoretically we could influence fragments with our intentions, allowing them to be absorbed into the field more quickly, if that's what we want. Our intentions are always much more powerful than we may be aware of. It's just a matter of time until these fragments disintegrate and are reabsorbed into the field.

PART 3

Healing Visualizations

*A*n overwhelming need for healing exists in our world. No one or two, or even several hundred, healers can meet the demand. One of my main goals is to remind people of their innate healing abilities and to teach them how to heal themselves. I urge you to ponder the ideas I've presented about the origin of the universe, our resulting oneness and our enormous energy-healing potential. We all have this built-in healing ability because of our connection to universal energy. We simply need to learn how to develop it and discipline ourselves to use it.

Energy healing is not magic. It is a real shift in a person's actual energy system, resulting in bodily changes occurring in real time. Healing is a process of change. The visualizations presented in this part of the book can be used for small aches and pains as well as for serious health challenges. The steps for each healing visualization are not hard. The concepts are simple. The visualizations are simple. The challenge is self-discipline. The challenge is setting aside time and actually doing the visualizations over a period of days, weeks and months. Then you will see the results.

The following words emphasize the main steps of self-healing:

The DreamHealer is within us.
DreamHealer, awaken!
Connect to yourself with healing intention.
Plant your vision of your future.
Grow it in your dream state.
Wake up to your new reality.

WHY DO VISUALIZATIONS?

Many people ask me, why do visualizations, specifically? I respond by telling them to take responsibility for their health by taking action. Think healthy, be healthy.

All of our attitudes and daily activities have a real physiological effect on our bodies. Our brains imprint an impression from visualizations we do, so they are processed as real events, even though they are created in our imaginations. This imprint sets off more electrical charges in the neurons of the brain. These signals flash between the synapses, which connect the neurons to one another. By repeating the visualizations regularly, the connections between neurons become stronger, more permanent and more accurate in making the visualizations realistic and our physical reaction to them real. Brain cells form a network. We can create a permanent pathway of change in our brains, which will create the beginning of a permanent memory adjustment in our bodies.

When I observe someone doing visualizations properly, I can see the flow of energy that they are directing within themselves. The impact on their physical self is indeed powerful. This is why I highly recommend visualizations: because I have seen their positive effects. One's own ability to influence oneself is an amazingly effective ability, and it can easily be harnessed with a few simple tools.

Think of yourself as a director creating a movie of your future—which then becomes your conscious reality. This is what you are doing by actively being in charge of your thoughts, words and deeds. Visualizations grant us this unlimited creative license.

Top athletes use visualization techniques because they realize that physical agility and skill is only a fraction of the game. In every sport, it is the psychological aspect that separates good athletes from great ones. The entire game plan is unfolding very precisely in the mind's eyes of top athletes of every sport. Optimal performance is just as much a psychological challenge as a physical one.

Each and every year, world records are broken. The record for the fastest runner in the world in the 1950s is now often broken by university track team members. What was once deemed an impossibly fast running speed is still admired but is no longer viewed as exceptional. Once records are broken, athletes know that increased performance is possible, and they believe they can do it. This is more of a psychological breakthrough than a physical one.

See yourself as you want to be. If you are an athlete, imagine with as much detail as you can what it feels like to wear that Olympic gold medal. See it, feel it, hear it, believe it. Make it real. Your body will respond to this as if it were the real event. Now you actually have a memory imprint that you have achieved this, and therefore you can do it again: You already know how to do it.

The same technique applies to healing visualizations. Imagine yourself doing all the things that you will be able to do once you achieve your goal of wellness. Make sure that your visualization is as detailed as possible as you imagine the physical challenges that you want to overcome. Do what you love to do once again. Envision this as if it is already your new reality.

It is vital that, as you do the visualizations, you sense them as being dynamic and fluid. Use all of your senses to imagine vividly the events happening to you, until your brain interprets these images as real experiences. Your brain will compute the information as if the thought is an event that is actually occurring. You will know that your visualizations are working when you start to feel changes in your health. Make your visualizations realistic with clear positive intention for optimal results. You are re-creating yourself in your new experience of wellness. Create your new healthy reality now. Remember that energy is being processed as new information within your body.

Your return to wellness is an ongoing learning process. The objective is not eternal life in our present form. Rather, the objective is to empower yourself to create an optimally functioning immune system, a balanced emotional state and a reawakening of your spiritual awareness.

Practice the exercises and visualizations in this book for a comprehensive lifestyle change. Incorporate visualizations into your daily routine and you will realize the advantages that they bring. Soon, doing them will be as natural as breathing. Enjoy your newfound sense of inner peace as you relax and grow in the mastery of this skill.

STRATEGIES TO ENHANCE
HEALING VISUALIZATIONS

Preparing yourself psychologically in order to get the maximum benefit from visualizations is essential. In many respects, doing visualizations is like painting a house. The first half is all preparation work. Filling all the small nail holes and cracks must be done first. This is followed by sanding and taping. It seems like forever before one gets to see the actual color of the new paint on the walls. We have all experienced what happens if we skip these meticulous preparation steps: The end result is not satisfactory because the improvement is flawed and doesn't last.

Likewise, to achieve long-lasting benefits from energy healing, we must realize that the groundwork *before* this journey is just as essential and time-consuming as the journey itself.

We can use our dreams most effectively by doing visualizations at bedtime. This is how we set them in our minds for the duration of our sleep. Our most imaginative state of mind is during our dream state. This is also our least judgmental phase, so visualizations will more easily become real to us and be processed as actual events at this time. Actively embed into your dream state a visualization that is most helpful to you and your well-being. You can accomplish this by thinking about a particular visualization as you drift off to sleep, so that it is rooted in your subconscious thoughts.

Breathing Exercise

Breathing effectively during your visualizations is important for providing oxygen, and hence energy, to all of your cells. You can easily do this by paying attention to your breathing in and out. Breathe in vital life energy and the mental picture will become more realistic.

Here is an easy two-step breathing exercise:

1. Inhale energy as deeply as possible, filling your lungs and abdominal cavity with air. Imagine when doing this that you are providing your body, mind and soul with everything you need to achieve your goal of wellness.
2. Strongly exhale the air from your lungs and abdominal cavity, releasing with it what you do not need or want in your body. In this way, rid your body of any emotional blockages and problems.

SPEED MEDITATION

To reach a calm, meditative state, most people prefer to be in quiet surroundings, with their body in a physically relaxed position. This is not always easy. We live such busy, stressful lives that there are often random thoughts in our heads or noises in our environment that prevent total quiet. The good news is that meditation can still be achieved, since this consciousness-expanding state originates in the mind. Environmental challenges such as noise and being physically uncomfortable will distract you only if you let them.

The means of entering the relaxed frame of mind that is meditation may vary, but what is important is that you are able to reach that level of calm consciousness vital for reflection. Once achieved, the quiet, altered state of mind operates in the same manner, no matter how it was reached.

Here is a meditation technique I use when my environment lacks physical comfort, calm and quiet. I call it speed meditation. The extreme sense of motion experienced during speed meditation causes confusion in our thought patterns, which disrupts our state of consciousness. This disruption in logic activates the subconscious mind, where calmness can be found.

1. Close your eyes and visualize in your mind's eye a merry-go-round. Visualize it as it sits motionless, capturing as much detail as you can. See the multi-colored roof and the stilled positions of the dancing animals.

2. Start up the motion. Watch the animals move up and down as the carousel spins around.

3. Increase the speed. Watch the animals go by faster and faster, concentrating on seeing as much detail as possible.

   Some people may find this dizzying until they get used to it. If you feel a little off balance, visualize the carousel rotating in the opposite direction. This will rebalance you. Then try increasing the speed again.

4. Take the speed to its limit. The carousel is moving as fast as you think it can go. No matter how fast it is spinning, keep accelerating the speed. This makes you visualize faster than the speed of your thoughts. You will feel a rush and will find yourself thinking of nothing. From this point onward, it is as if the carousel spins beyond conscious awareness.

This heightened state of awareness through the visualization of speed at the breaking point leads to a peaceful and relaxed feeling. The mind-body resets itself into a frame of consciousness in which a meditative state can quickly and easily follow.

MAXIMIZING FOCUSED INTENTION

Now that your beliefs, intentions and expectations are aligned toward your healing, the next step is to know that you are ready, willing and able to implement self-healing. Information is constantly being exchanged between your quantum hologram and your physical self. Visualizations are tools you can use to be in control of this information exchange process. You know where to direct your immune system for optimum performance. Visualizations enable you to reset yourself to your own maximum capacity for accomplishing this.

Visualizations, when done with clear intention and detailed focus, incorporate all five senses into a dynamic and realistic feeling of experiencing the event. What you envision in your mind's eye with the vividness of a true experience triggers your subconscious mind into action. This maximizes your focused intentions in order to optimally guide your immune system in correcting the problem.

Chronic problems are often no longer recognized by your body as difficulties because it has become accustomed to them. They are often overlooked or ignored so that your body can concentrate on the new incoming information. Visualizations can reawaken your body to the awareness that there is a problem so that your immune system can respond. Your unwavering intention to change an unhealthy status quo will activate a shift in the subconscious mind.

Expand on your visualizations to include all of your senses. People have different dominant senses, so some may find it more realistic to hear their visualizations. Others may find that they can feel the visualizations more accurately and realistically than they can see them. Some people find that if they narrate aloud what is happening, it makes a more lasting impression, so they speak it. Self-talk can help boost self-confidence in this process of self-creation. These approaches, whether dramatic or reserved, are all equally valid and effective as long as they are meaningful to you. Trust yourself.

If you find that your mind wanders when you are visualizing, stop and relax. Refresh your screen, so to speak. This process involves reprogramming your mind and body. Be patient with yourself. Concentrate on the feeling and it will return. Refocus.

EXERCISE FOR PROJECTING A HOLOGRAPHIC IMAGE

A hologram, as noted earlier, is a three-dimensional projection containing all of the information (past, present and future) of a person, place or thing (see Illustrations 18 and 19). A person's optimal state of health is contained within it. It is not necessary to master this exercise in order to do visualizations, as you can imagine doing any visualization directly on your body. Using this holographic image is optional for self-healing, but it is useful. With practice, as you become more skilled, you may even find it most effective to visualize directing energy onto both your body and your projected image simultaneously. It is necessary to at least be familiar with projecting an image before assisting others with their healing.

The first few times you practice this exercise, you will find it easier to visualize a simple two-dimensional image rather than the actual three-dimensional image. With practice, your intuition and intention will connect you to more information, until you are linking to the hologram itself.

1. Stand in front of a full-length mirror and take a careful look at your reflection. Try to remember every detail of your image—all your physical characteristics.
2. Close your eyes and burn this image of yourself into your mind's eye.
3. With eyes closed, project this two-dimensional image of yourself about two feet in front of you, as a base for your visualizations. This image of your body can be any size, though two feet in height is typical.
4. Through your visualizations, direct energy flow onto this image for optimal health.

You can also direct healing visualizations to others as follows:

1. Look at a photograph of the person's face.
2. Concentrate on the person's physical characteristics as you close your eyes and burn the image into your memory.
3. With eyes closed, project a hologram in front of you.
4. Direct the energy flow through visualizations with your focused intention to achieve optimal health.
5. Dispose of the person's energy blockages by throwing them into a vacuum, the garbage or a black hole. Energy blockages

need a host organism in order to thrive; without one, they dissipate quickly.

SPECIFIC VISUALIZATIONS

It is important to remember that the following visualizations are guidelines only; they are meant for you to tailor to your individual needs. It would be impossible to cover here visualizations for every ailment. This is where your imagination is of the utmost importance; set your imagination free to reach what you desire. Adjust the visualizations in whatever ways will most efficiently and effectively heal the ailment. Experiment with them, and modify them to suit you. Be creative. Think of them as clothes that you can change into and out of to adapt to any occasion. If white light is too hot for you, try a cooler color such as blue or purple. Perhaps your mythical dragon (discussed below) breathes out red flames. Play with images and experiment. This also keeps visualizations alive, dynamic and exciting.

Do the research necessary to find out what your problem looks like anatomically. Also find out what the optimally healthy functioning of this area looks like—this is what you are striving for. Build your personal visualization from this information. In this sense, it is important to make your visualizations as realistic as possible to you, so the images you use should be as realistic as possible.

It doesn't matter if you are standing, sitting or lying down when you do the visualizations, as long as you are comfortable. The main thing is to relax and focus your intentions on what you expect to achieve. The primary factors in all healing strategies, including the visualizations, are your attitudes and intentions. Be confident as you set out to master your new skills.

Light-Hearted Visualization

For any condition, but especially for self-love and acceptance, and mending a broken heart (see Illustration 20)

An effective general visualization, which can be modified for all conditions, is the ball of bright white light. This exercise makes maximum use of the heart's ability to synchronize universal energy available to the body, mind and spirit.

Many people have written to me about having a broken heart. I have recommended that they do the light-hearted visualization, and they report wonderful results. In fact, it is effective for all matters of the heart, especially when we need to increase love and acceptance of ourselves.

Increase your love for yourself and the result will be increased self-confidence in your ability to transform yourself. To know you can do it is an essential step on your journey to success. As you experience greater self-acceptance and deeper knowing, you effectively begin to reprogram your mind and body.

This visualization pulls universal energy into your body through the top of your head and collects it in the area of your heart. Your heart amplifies the intensity of energy, and it is near your body's core, which makes its distribution to all other areas of the body easy.

1. With inhalation, imagine bringing in the sunlight through the top of your head and into your heart.
2. Breathe in several times, collecting all of that light in your heart area.
3. Imagine your heart is the sun, radiating out beams of pure light energy. Be the sun.
4. With exhalation, radiate that warmth and love to every part of yourself. See and feel yourself literally shine from within. This opens your heart to universal energy, to your own energy and to the energy of everyone and everything else.
5. Feel the strength as you become unified with everything. Experience the energy of peace and harmony.

See your heart radiating as brightly as the sun.
Feel yourself glow with energy.
Hear your heart pumping.
Smell and taste the heat.
Make it real.

Lightbulb Visualization

For illnesses that affect or have spread to the entire body, such as infection, cancer and AIDS (see Illustration 21)

As I obtain more experience and practice, I am able to incorporate more specific visualizations into my healing. In workshops I have held, there have been many requests for visualizations to deal with illnesses that affect, or have spread to, the entire body, such as AIDS and cancer. An effective visualization for healing such an illness is one that recruits every cell in the body to recognize the problem. The lightbulb visualization does this.

1. With inhalation, bring in universal energy through the top of your head. (See the Bring in Universal Energy exercise in Chapter 4.)

2. Imagine every cell as a magnet, attracting energy into each cell.

3. Let light energy radiate out to every cell. Imagine filling every cell with light until every cell becomes so bright that each looks like an individual lightbulb, radiating its own light.

4. Imagine shaking your entire body like one of those vibrating belts that promise to jiggle away excess fat. With every shake, the individual cells begin to reach a similar frequency, until they are all resonating at the same coherent vibration. If you look in a mirror, your aura will be almost too bright to see your reflection.

5. Visualize your entire body as a guitar resonating with a single harmonious chord strummed in perfect tune. When your entire body resonates in harmony, you no longer see every cell as an individual light but the entire body as one

continuous body of light. Every cell in your body is now working together toward the common goal of fixing the problem.

See your entire being light up.
Feel your harmonic flow of energy.
Hear your single resonating frequency.
Smell and taste the vapors.
Make it real.

Once all the cells are resonating at the same frequency, there is cooperation between cells, enabling you to more effectively communicate with your cells. Any visualization is more intense and effective when cell communication coherence is achieved. You may also find it effective to talk to your body as you guide yourself through the visualizations. Saying the steps aloud may help, especially when you first start doing them.

If you have cancer, imagine every cell in your body recognizing the problem and attacking it. Do not limit this visualization solely to immune system cells. Every cell must be included, even skin cells. Every cell has the ability to give at least some resistance to any illness. Getting every cell in your body working together creates a powerful force to eliminate the problem and simultaneously boost your immune system.

When a person with cancer undergoes chemotherapy and that treatment doesn't work, he or she is often dealt a double whammy. The cancer remains active, yet the chemotherapy has compromised the person's immune system. It is not uncommon to have a very low white blood cell count after several sessions of chemotherapy. The person's primary health challenge now becomes restoring a functioning immune system and, second, eliminating the cancer. No matter what your condition or what therapy you are pursuing, it is important to focus on rebuilding your immune system, since it is your primary source of health and well-being.

Even if you do not know exactly what your health problem is or do not have a clear idea as to how your body could heal, it is still useful to practice the lightbulb visualization. Just imagine speaking to your cells as if you were speaking to a person. Tell the cells to find the problem and eliminate it. However, ideally, the visualization should be anatomically accurate. I therefore highly recommend that you research the illness and understand exactly what your problem looks like, and exactly what the area should look like when the problem is gone. Be sure to maximize your healing potential by improving your immune defenses too.

This lightbulb visualization is also effective for emotionally based illnesses. Any problem you have, even if it is emotion based, has a physical effect on your body because of the various biochemicals that are released. When speaking to the cells involved in an emotional problem, imagine every cell in your body forgetting past emotions that are still causing you harm.

Every cell essentially has its own memory, and you are simply telling each cell to release painful emotional memories.

Light Injections Visualization

For any condition that affects one target area, such as a specific organ; also for arthritis and pain (see Illustration 22)

Use this visualization for any localized health challenge, such as a specific organ. It can also be used for arthritis, pain issues and sports injuries. Many acute and chronic pains occur in specific areas, so they can be addressed individually. If you have several areas you want to work on, use this visualization on one area at a time.

1. Visualize filling a syringe with pure, white light.
2. Imagine injecting this pure white light into your problem area. As light fills the area, light glows and radiates from within.
3. As the surrounding tissues soak up the light, you will shine in wellness.

See your problem dissolving into the pure light.
Feel your calm energy ripple.
Hear your light radiating.
Smell and taste the energy.
Make it real.

Bright White Light Visualization

For connecting to your inner self (see Illustration 23)

When I connect directly to the bright white light that is at the center of the brain, I experience an incredible sense of connectedness. I see an image of the body in perfect health. Everyone has a problem of some sort—an old injury or an injury forming. The image inside the bright white light has no signs of any illness or injury of any kind. As I mentioned earlier, this is the area many people refer to as the soul.

The soul is the glue that unifies the energy systems of each cell into a coherent frequency that is consistent with the whole person. It is what keeps each cell working in unison with all others. Even though every cell interacts with its environment and has a consciousness, the soul represents our singular consciousness, observer of all of our experiences. It is what each of us refers to as "I"; it is the self, the observer.

Many conclusions could be drawn as to what this white light is; all interpretations would arise from our personal biased meanings. I perceive this white light as containing an image of perfect health—as the original perfect blueprint. It is this image of perfect health that we all strive to experience. I believe that the image of perfect health is in you. Your optimal image is what is looking out of your eyes at this very moment.

Many specific visualizations can be done utilizing this bright white light. People have found working with it to be especially effective for emotional illnesses.

1. With inhalation, bring energy from the universe in through the top of your head. (See the Bring in Universal Energy exercise in Chapter 4.) Collect and focus it at the center of your brain.

2. Light the center of your brain with your internal light source and watch it glow.

3. With exhalation, visualize light energy roots growing out of the bright white light.

4. Grow the roots and expand their network until every cell in your body is connected to these roots.

5. See pulses of light going from the center of your brain to every cell along these pathways as your body messages synchronize. With each pulse of light, you can see your problems or illness shattering like glass and falling away from your body forever.

See your light pulsing.
Feel your perfect self.
Hear your problems shattering.
Smell and taste the purity of energy.
Make it real.

The light from the center of your brain has effectively flushed out the old program about your health challenge and reverted to the original default image of your perfect self.

Bubble Wrap Visualization

For a localized problem, such as a tumor or fibroid, anywhere in the body (see Illustration 24)

Most of us have popped bubble wrap at one time or another; this visualization makes use of that experience. This visualization is useful when one wants to rid the body of something foreign that is in one location, such as a tumor or fibroid.

1. Imagine the problem area as layers of bubble wrap.
2. Move your focused intention to that location.
3. With inhalation, breathe fresh air and healing light energy into all the pockets of the bubble wrap, filling them nearly to the breaking point.
4. With exhalation, pop as many bubbles as you can. Imagine tightening your muscles in that area to make it happen.
5. Repeat the steps until every bubble has burst.
6. Exhale with force in order to expel all of the unwanted material from your body. Fill yourself with boundless healing energy.

See your bubbles pop.
Feel the rush of air as they burst.
Hear each mini-explosion.
Smell and taste pristine air.
Make it real.

Mythical Dragon Breathing Visualization

For eliminating stress (see Illustration 25)

This exercise can be very useful for the elimination of stress held tightly within your body. Focus on the area of your body where you are holding all of your worries.

1. With inhalation, imagine that you are breathing in white, hot flames.
2. Focus on moving these flames with your awareness to your place of stress.
3. With exhalation, breathe out the flames and the ashes of your burned out stress.
4. With each successive breath, move your awareness lower in your body, until the flames shoot from the ground up. Each breath in fans the coals. Each breath out eliminates body tightness or stress.

See flames engulf your stress.
Feel ashes exit your body.
Hear your breath release it.
Smell and taste the smoke.
Make it real.

Reflection

Every thought and intention we emit is energy. When you throw a stone in the ocean, the ripples affect every atom in the ocean. When we think good intentions or thoughts toward someone, we affect everyone around us and beyond. Imagine what kind of a world this would be if we all had good thoughts and intentions. Such a world is possible if we all teach one another about the influence we have on ourselves and others. When the world comes to this understanding, there will be no wars and no killings, only harmony. Like the cells in our bodies, we all will be working together.

I see this as a realistic objective because I continue to receive countless emails from people who understand this interconnectedness we all share. Meanwhile, there remains the challenge of knocking down the many walls of fear that remain throughout the world. There are many people who have a strong awareness of our connection with one another but have had to suppress their abilities because of fear of ridicule. Yet, everywhere I see evidence that this wall of fear is eroding.

Self-empowerment spreads as we learn how we can influence our reality. Self-empowerment is contagious as each person passes on to others the knowledge of what we all are capable of achieving. There is a wave of understanding and acceptance of our interconnectedness and healing ability that is building. The momentum of this wave is increasing exponentially. Each of us can speed the process of change with our own unique gifts. Let us all hold this vision of a world that is healed.

Stay tuned!

Acknowledgments

Thank you to Doris Lora for her inspiration and patience. Thanks to Robert Stirling for his inquisitiveness. He brought forward lots of questions, which are answered in this book. Many thanks to Ivan Rados for his exquisite art creations. Thanks to everyone who has supported and helped me on this journey.

DreamHealer

For information about workshops,
newsletters and ordering the DVD

DreamHealer Visualizations for Self-Empowerment

visit **www.dreamhealer.com**